# DESSERT TEMPTATIONS

**50 deliciously inviting
recipes for every occasion**

# DESSERT TEMPTATIONS

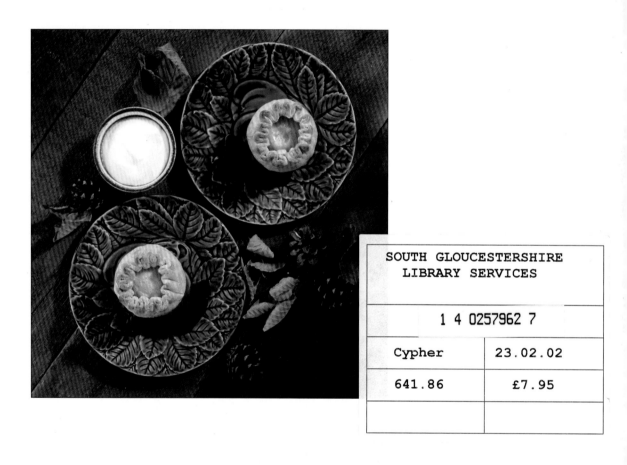

**Consultant Editor: Jenni Fleetwood**

**southwater**

This edition is published by Southwater

Distributed in the UK by
The Manning Partnership
251–253 London Road East
Batheaston
Bath BA1 7RL
tel. 01225 852 727
fax 01225 852 852

Published in the USA by
Anness Publishing Inc.
27 West 20th Street
Suite 504
New York
NY 10011
fax 212 807 6813

Distributed in Canada by
General Publishing
895 Don Mills Road
400–402 Park Centre
Toronto, Ontario M3C 1W3
tel. 416 445 3333
fax 416 445 5991

Distributed in Australia by
Sandstone Publishing
Unit 1, 360 Norton Street
Leichhardt
New South Wales 2040
tel. 02 9560 7888
fax 02 9560 7488

Southwater is an imprint of Anness Publishing Limited
Hermes House, 88–89 Blackfriars Road, London SE1 8HA
tel. 020 7401 2077; fax 020 7633 9499

© 1997, 2001 Anness Publishing Limited

*Publisher*: Joanna Lorenz
*Senior Editor*: Linda Fraser
*Editor*: Margaret Malone
*Designer*: Lilian Lindblom
*Jacket design*: The Bridgewater Book Company Limited
*Photographers*: Karl Adamson, Edward Allwright, Steve Baxter, James Duncan,
Amanda Heywood, Tim Hill and Don Last
*Recipes*: Alex Barker, Carla Capalbo, Chritine France, Sarah Gates, Shirley Gill,
Patricia Lousada, Norma MacMillan, Sue Maggs, Sarah Maxwell, Janice Murfitt,
Angela Nilsen, Hilaire Walden, Laura Washburn, Steven Wheeler and
Elizabeth Wolf-Cohen

For all recipes, quantities are given in both metric and imperial measures, and
where appropriate, measures are given in standard cups and spoons. Follow
one set, but not a mixture, because they are not interchangeable.

Previously published as *Step-by-Step 50 Traditional Rich Puddings*

1 3 5 7 9 10 8 6 4 2

# CONTENTS

# INTRODUCTION

Why is it that some puddings flare into fashion for a year or two, only to sink without trace, while others endure for generations? Perhaps at least part of the secret is simplicity. There are a few elaborate desserts – usually made to mark special occasions – but the majority of puddings that remain popular have a relatively small number of ingredients and a cooking method that can be summed up in a few words. They are the sort of recipes that are handed down from parent to child, often on tatty scraps of paper or copied from hand-written notebooks. Bread and Butter Pudding, Jam Tart, Apple Brown Betty and Baked Rice Pudding are typical examples that have stood the test of time.

Sharing favourite recipes is a time-honoured custom, which explains why so many dishes native to one country turn up in another. British favourites like Summer Pudding have their parallels across the Atlantic, while French specialities such as Crème Caramel are now regarded as international treats, as is Australia's Pavlova.

Some recipes have changed little over the centuries, while others have evolved. Our recipe for Chocolate Tiramisu, which has a pastry case rather than the original coffee-soaked biscuits, is one example.

The collection includes a couple of the 'new traditionals': recipes whose origins are relatively recent, but which have all the elements that point to perpetual success. Ginger and Banana Brûlée is one such, as is the hugely popular Banoffee Pie.

The saying that the proof of the pudding is in the eating, is as true as it ever was, so tuck in and enjoy these delicious treats.

# Good Things in Store

Many traditional puddings use simple store-cupboard ingredients. This page provides an at-a-glance checklist for stocking up.

## The pudding pantry

• plain and self-raising white and wholemeal flour; also cornflour
• raising agents: baking powder; bicarbonate of soda; cream of tartar; easy-blend dried yeast
• cocoa powder
• skimmed milk powder; condensed milk; evaporated milk; coconut milk
• granulated sugar; soft light and soft dark brown sugars; caster sugar; icing sugar
• porridge oats; sponge fingers; biscuits for crumb crusts; semolina and tapioca; short-grain (pudding) rice

• dried fruit: sultanas; raisins; currants; dates; mixed peel; ready-to-use dried apricots and prunes; mixed fruit; also glacé cherries and crystallized ginger
• sweet spices such as cinnamon, ground mixed spice, cloves, allspice, star anise, cardamom and nutmeg; also vanilla pods
• natural vanilla essence; rose water; orange flower water
• nuts, especially almonds, walnuts, pecans and hazelnuts
• jams and conserves; honey; golden syrup; maple syrup; black treacle; fruit spreads
• powdered gelatine and packet jellies
• dark and plain chocolate

## From the fridge

• butter and margarine
• cottage cheese; soft cheeses such as ricotta and mascarpone; also fromage frais
• single, double and whipping cream; also crème fraîche
• eggs (bring to room temperature before using)
• natural yogurt; Greek-style yogurt

# Equipment

Traditional puddings do not require elaborate gadgetry – any reasonably well-equipped kitchen will suffice. Here's a list of the bare essentials, plus some invaluable extras.

## Basic essentials

• bowls in various sizes. Heatproof glass bowls are useful for melting chocolate. Old-fashioned pudding basins can double as mixing bowls
• ramekins for individual mousses and cream pots; also useful for sponging gelatine
• decorative moulds for jellies and set creams; dariole moulds
• baking tins, preferably non-stick: both round and square
• measures: kitchen scales; set of measuring spoons; measuring jugs

• citrus zester for removing the rind from oranges, lemons and limes; canelle knife for decorating fruit; lemon squeezer; apple corer; peeler
• grater with different-sized serrations; also nutmeg grater
• sieve for sifting dry ingredients and sieving fruit purées
• rolling pin, pastry blender (optional) and pastry brush
• chopping boards (polypropylene for preference)
• balloon whisk for whisking egg whites, whipping cream and beating sauces by hand; electric

whisk for those without strong wrists
• wooden spoons for creaming ingredients; honey twirl for using honey without mess; slotted draining spoon; rubber spatula for scraping mixtures from bowls
• food processor: not essential but very useful for puréeing fruit, making pastry and crumbing biscuits for crusts
• ice cream maker (optional); ice cream scoop

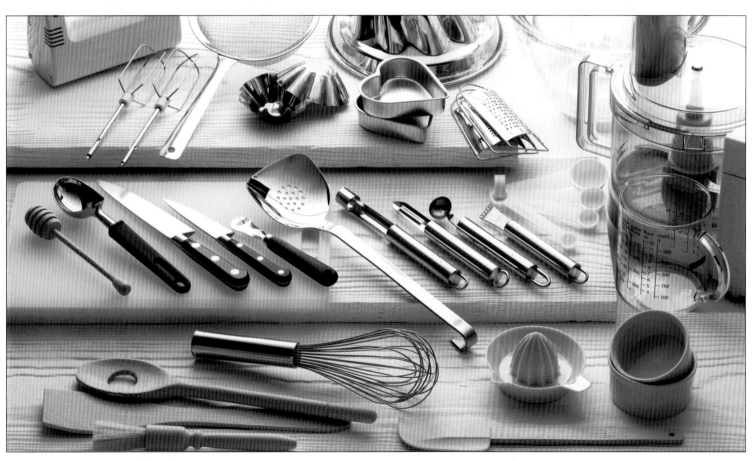

# TECHNIQUES

## Making Shortcrust Pastry

The secret of making successful shortcrust is not to overwork the dough. Use a light, swift touch when rubbing in the fat.

**1** Sift 225 g/8 oz/2 cups plain flour and 1.5 ml/¼ tsp salt into a bowl. Add 115 g/4 oz/½ cup mixed diced butter and margarine. Rub in with your fingertips until the mixture resembles breadcrumbs.

**2** Sprinkle over 45 ml/3 tbsp iced water. Toss gently with a fork to moisten, then press the dough into a ball, adding about 15 ml/1 tbsp more water if necessary. Wrap in clear film and chill for 30 minutes.

**3** If using a food processor, mix the flour, salt and cubed fat in the bowl, then pulse until the mixture is crumbed. Add the iced water and pulse until the dough starts to clump together. Remove from the processor, shape into a ball, wrap in clear film and chill.

## Lining a Tin with Pastry

Let the chilled pastry soften slightly at room temperature before rolling it out on a surface lightly dusted with flour.

**1** Using even pressure, roll out the pastry to the same shape as your tin, but about 5 cm/2 in larger all around. Roll the dough in one direction only. Lift it and turn it occasionally to stop it from sticking to the surface.

**2** Gently place the pastry over the rolling pin, place it over the tin and gently unroll it so that the pastry drops into the tin. Keep the dough central and avoid stretching it if you can.

**3** Using your fingertips, lift and ease the pastry into the tin, gently pressing it over the bottom and up the sides. Trim the dough to leave a 1 cm/½ in overhang, then turn the excess under to strengthen the rim.

# Finishing the Edge

Give a pastry case a fancy finish by decorating the rim. For a simple pattern, simply mark the rim with the tines of a fork.

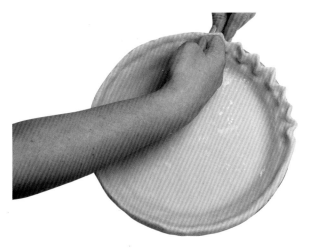

**1** **Crimped edge:** Put the knuckle or tip of an index finger inside the pastry case, pointing directly out, then use your other index finger and thumb to pinch the dough around your index finger to make a v-shape. Continue around the pastry rim.

**2** **Cutout edge:** Trim the dough even with the rim and press it flat. Cut out small shapes from the pastry trimmings. Moisten the rim of the pastry case with egg wash or milk, then press the cutouts carefully but firmly in place.

**3** **Ribbon edge:** Trim the dough even with the rim and press it flat. Cut long pastry strips about 2 cm/¾ in wide. Moisten the rim of the pastry case with egg wash or milk, press on one end of a pastry strip, then twist the strip gently and press it on to the edge again. Continue around the pastry rim.

# Baking Blind

Partly or fully cooking pastry cases before adding moist fillings helps to keep them crisp. The technique is called baking blind.

**1** Cut out a greaseproof paper or foil circle about 7.5 cm/3 in larger all around than the pastry case. Prick the bottom of the pastry case with a fork, then ease in the paper or foil circle.

**2** Preheat the oven to 200°C/400°F/ Gas 6. Cover the bottom of the lined pastry shell with dried beans kept especially for this purpose, or use ceramic baking beans, making a neat, even layer.

**3** For partly cooked pastry, bake the pastry case for 15–20 minutes, then lift out the paper and beans. For fully baked pastry, remove the paper and beans after 15 minutes, then bake the empty case for 5–10 minutes more, until golden. Cool before filling.

# Making a Biscuit Case

Biscuit cases are very easy to make. Use digestive biscuits, gingernuts or shortbread, with grated lemon rind or nutmeg if you like.

**1** Combine 225 g/8 oz/2 cups crushed digestive biscuits with 115 g/4 oz/½ cup melted butter. Add 45–60 ml/3–4 tbsp caster sugar, if required. Stir well to mix.

**2** Tip the mixture into a greased 20 cm/8 in springform cake tin. Spread it over the bottom and up the side, then use a spoon or your fingers to pack the crumbs into an even crust.

**3** Either put the biscuit case in the fridge to chill for about an hour until set, or bake it at 180°C/350°F/Gas 4 for 8–10 minutes. Cool before filling.

# Preparing Nuts

Nuts are a popular pudding ingredient, either whole or ground. They may be stirred into a mixture or used for decoration.

**1** **Blanching almonds:** Put the nuts in a bowl and pour over boiling water to cover. Leave for 2 minutes, then drain the nuts, cool slightly, and squeeze to pop them out of their skins.

**2** **Roasting nuts:** Spread the nuts on a baking sheet. Either roast in a preheated oven at 180°C/350°F/Gas 4 or under a moderate grill. Shake the sheet occasionally and remove the nuts as soon as they are golden brown.

**3** **Grinding nuts:** Grind small batches in a nut mill or clean coffee grinder, removing them as soon as they are fine. A food processor can be used but take care not to process the nuts to a paste.

# Preparing Fruit

Fruit features widely in both hot and cold pudding recipes, either as a main ingredient or in a filling or sauce.

# Making Apricot Glaze

Apricot glaze gives fruit toppings or fillings a lovely, shiny appearance. The lemon juice intensifies the flavour.

**1** **Making citrus shreds:** Thinly pare the rind from a lemon, orange or lime. Cut the rind into strips, then into very fine shreds. Boil the shreds for a couple of minutes in water or syrup to soften them and reduce their bitterness.

**2** **Stringing currants:** Pull red, black or white currants through the tines of a fork so that the currants pop off, leaving the stalks behind. If currants are to be frozen, freeze them on the stalk; frozen ones come off easily.

**1** Place a few spoonfuls of apricot jam in a small pan. Add a squeeze of lemon juice. Heat the jam, stirring until it has melted and is runny.

**3** **Hulling strawberries:** Use a special huller to remove the leafy green top and central core, or cut these out with a small sharp knife.

**2** Pour the melted jam into a wire sieve set over a bowl. Stir the jam with a wooden spoon to help it go through.

**3** Return the strained jam to the pan and warm it through gently. Keep the glaze warm and brush it generously over the fruit until it is evenly coated.

# Melting Chocolate

Melting chocolate requires patience and care, but the process is very simple. It can be done over hot water or in a microwave oven.

**1** To microwave, break 115 g/4 oz plain chocolate into small pieces. Place it in a heatproof bowl and cook on medium (50% power) for 2 minutes. Milk and white chocolate should be melted for the same time, but on low (30% power). Stir well.

**2** To melt chocolate over hot water, bring a small saucepan of water to the boil. Turn off the heat and place the bowl of chocolate over the hot water. The bowl must not touch the water, nor should any drops of water be allowed to fall into the chocolate or it will become grainy.

**3** Leave the chocolate until very soft, then stir it lightly. Melted chocolate is used in many puddings and can also be used for dipping strawberries or physalis. Drizzled chocolate makes a simple, but excellent, decoration.

# Piping Cream or Meringue

Piping is an art that anyone can master with a little practice. All it takes is a steady hand and even pressure.

**1** Select the right nozzle – a star for a rosette, for instance, or a small, plain nozzle for writing – and attach to the bag. Hold the piping bag open with your hand, half-fill it, then twist it closed, at the same time expelling any trapped air.

**2** Hold the bag firmly in one hand, with your fingers around the twisted section. Use the other hand to lightly guide the nozzle. Exert a very firm, steady pressure and start to pipe.

**3** The trick with piping is to keep the pressure steady until the swirl or other design is complete. A sudden squeeze will produce a large blob rather than an even flow. As soon as the design is finished, stop applying pressure, push down slightly and quickly lift up the nozzle.

# Making a Batter

The texture of a batter depends on its purpose. This one is perfect for pancakes, but a thicker one would be required for coating.

**1** Sift 175 g/6 oz/1½ cups plain flour into a mixing bowl. Stir in 10 ml/2 tsp caster sugar. Make a well in the centre of the mixture and add 2 eggs and 150 ml/¼ pint/⅔ cup milk.

**2** Beat the eggs and milk well, gradually drawing in the surrounding dry ingredients until the mixture is smooth. Stir in a further 300 ml/½ pint/1¼ cups milk, together with 25 g/1 oz/2 tbsp melted butter.

**3** For a very light batter, separate the eggs and add only the yolks with the milk. Whisk the whites in a grease-free bowl until they form soft peaks when the whisk is removed. Fold them into the batter just before use.

# Making Pancakes

A pancake batter should have the consistency of whipping cream. If it is at all lumpy, strain it. Leave to stand for 20 minutes before use.

**1** Heat a 20 cm/8 in pancake pan, then grease it lightly with melted butter. Pour in 45–60 ml/3–4 tbsp batter (see recipe left), then quickly tilt the pan so that the batter spreads to cover the bottom thinly and evenly.

**2** Cook the pancake for 30–45 seconds, until it has set. Lift the edge with a palette knife; the base of the pancake should have browned lightly. Shake the pan to loosen the pancake, then turn or flip it over.

**3** Cook the other side for about 30 seconds, then slide the pancake out. Make more pancakes in the same way, then spread them with your chosen filling before rolling them or folding them into triangles.

# BASIC RECIPES

## How to Make a Steamed Sponge Pudding

Light and lovely, old-fashioned steamed pudding
is a treat, especially with a jam topping trickling
down the sides.

*Serves 4*

INGREDIENTS
30 ml/2 tbsp jam (optional)
115 g/4 oz/½ cup butter, plus
    extra for greasing
115 g/4 oz/½ cup caster sugar
2 eggs, lightly beaten
175 g/6 oz/1½ cups self-raising
    flour, sifted

**1** Grease a 1.2 litre/2 pint/5 cup pudding basin. Spoon in the jam, if using, or fit a disc of buttered greaseproof paper in the bottom. Beat the butter and sugar until creamy.

**2** Beat in the eggs with a little flour. Fold in the remaining flour. Spoon the mixture into the basin, filling it two-thirds full. Lay a disc of buttered greaseproof paper on top.

**3** Lay a piece of greaseproof paper on a piece of foil. Holding the paper and foil together, fold a 2.5 cm/1 in pleat across the centre (this will expand so that the pudding can rise).

**5** To cover with a cloth instead of foil, use a cotton square three times larger than the top of the basin. Lay it over the greased paper, pleat the top and secure it with string. Bring up opposite corners and knot securely.

**6** Place a trivet or upturned saucer in a saucepan or roasting tin. Add the pudding and half-fill the pan with water and bring to the boil. Cover tightly with a lid or foil. If using a saucepan, set over a moderate heat on top of the hob, or place the roasting tin into a preheated 180°C/350°F/Gas 4 oven. Steam for 1½–2 hours, topping up the water as needed. Turn out and serve.

**4** Centre the paper and foil over the pudding and tie securely under the rim with string. Trim off the foil corners neatly with scissors.

# How to Make a Soufflé Omelette

This cross between a pancake and a soufflé starts cooking on top of the stove and finishes in the oven or under the grill.

*Serves 2*

INGREDIENTS
4 eggs, separated
75 g/3 oz/6 tbsp caster sugar
pinch of cream of tartar
  (optional)
melted butter for greasing
sweetened fruit purée for filling

**1** Preheat the oven to 180°C/350°F/ Gas 4. Put the egg yolks in a mixing bowl. Add the caster sugar and beat with an electric whisk until thick and pale.

**2** Whisk the egg whites in a grease-free bowl until they hold stiff peaks. If you are not using a copper bowl, whisk in the cream of tartar.

**3** Using a rubber spatula, fold the whites into the yolk mixture as lightly as possible, using a figure-of-eight action.

**4** Heat a 23 cm/9 in pancake pan that can be used safely in the oven. Grease it generously with melted butter. When hot, pour in the egg mixture.

**5** Reduce the heat to low and cook the omelette without stirring for 5 minutes until puffy and set around the edges, but still soft in the centre.

**6** Transfer the pan to the oven and bake for 3–5 minutes until the top is set and lightly browned. Spread with the filling, fold in half and serve.

*17*

# How to Make a Fruit Crumble

This traditional pudding, consisting of baked fruit
with a sweet crumble topping, is a sure winner
and very easy to make.

*Serves 4*

INGREDIENTS
800 g/1¾ lb pears or apples
50 g/2 oz/¼ cup caster sugar
30 ml/2 tbsp plain flour

FOR THE CRUMBLE TOPPING
115 g/4 oz/1 cup plain flour
150 g/5 oz/scant 1 cup soft light
    brown sugar
5 ml/1 tsp ground ginger or
    cinnamon
115 g/4 oz/½ cup butter, diced
50 g/2 oz/½ cup chopped
    walnuts (optional)

**1** Preheat the oven to 190°C/375°F/
Gas 5. Make the topping. Mix the flour
and sugar in a bowl. Add ginger if using
pears; cinnamon if using apples.

**2** Cut or rub in the butter until the
mixture resembles breadcrumbs, then
stir in the walnuts, if using. Set the
crumble aside.

**3** Peel and core the pears or apples.
Slice them thinly. If not using at once,
drop into water with lemon juice added
to stop the fruit from turning brown.

**4** Drain the fruit if necessary and put it in a bowl. Add the sugar and flour and toss
well. Spread the mixture evenly in a baking dish.

**5** Scatter the crumble mixture on top
so that the fruit is covered in a neat,
even layer.

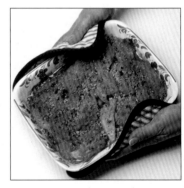

**6** Bake for 25–30 minutes or until the
fruit is tender and the topping is golden
brown and crisp. Serve warm, with
whipped cream, soured cream, yogurt or
ice cream.

# How to Make a Swiss Roll

A light, luscious Swiss Roll makes a superb sweet. Master the art of making and rolling the sponge and compliments are sure to follow.

*Serves 6–8*

INGREDIENTS
3 eggs
115 g/4 oz/½ cup caster sugar,
    plus extra for sprinkling
75 g/3 oz/¾ cup plain flour
15 ml/1 tbsp boiling water
90 g/6 tbsp apricot, peach or
    strawberry jam

**1** Preheat the oven to 200°C/400°F/ Gas 6. Line and grease a 33 x 23 cm/ 13 x 9 in Swiss roll tin. Using an electric whisk, beat the eggs and caster sugar in a bowl until pale and so thick that when the beaters are lifted, their trail remains for at least 15 seconds.

**2** Sift the flour over the surface. Carefully fold it in with a large metal spoon, then add the boiling water in the same way.

**3** Spoon the mixture into the prepared tin, spread evenly into the corners and level the surface. Bake for 10–12 minutes, until the cake springs back when lightly pressed.

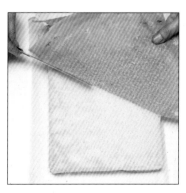

**4** Spread a sheet of greaseproof paper on a flat surface, sprinkle it with caster sugar, then invert the cake on top. Peel off the lining paper.

**5** Neatly trim the edges of the cake. Make a neat cut two-thirds of the way through the cake, about 1 cm/½ in from the short edge nearest you.

**6** Spread the cake with the jam and roll up quickly from the partially cut end. Hold in position for a minute, making sure the join is underneath. Cool on a wire rack.

# How to Make a Basic Custard

A home-made custard is a luscious sauce for hot and cold puddings, and is also the basis for a creamy, rich ice cream.

*Makes about 475 ml/ 16 fl oz/2 cups*

INGREDIENTS
450 ml/¾ pint/scant 2 cups milk
1 vanilla pod, split lengthways
4 egg yolks
50 g/2 oz/¼ cup caster sugar,
    plus extra for sprinkling

**1** Put the milk in a heavy-based saucepan. Hold the vanilla pod over the pan and scrape the tiny seeds into the milk, then add the split pod.

**2** Heat the milk until bubbles appear around the edge. Remove from the heat, cover and set aside to infuse for 10 minutes. Lift out the vanilla pod.

**3** In a bowl, beat the egg yolks with the sugar until smoothly blended and creamy. Gradually add the hot milk, stirring all the time.

**4** Pour the mixture into the top of a double boiler or a heatproof bowl. Set over a pan of barely simmering water and heat gently, stirring constantly.

**5** Continue to cook for 12–15 minutes, stirring with a wooden spoon, until the custard thickens to a creamy consistency that coats the spoon.

**6** Strain the custard into a bowl and serve. If using cold, sprinkle a little caster sugar over the surface to prevent the formation of a skin.

## COOK'S TIPS
• For a richer custard, use cream or a mixture of milk and cream.
• Use 5 ml/1 tsp vanilla essence instead of the vanilla pod, if you prefer. Omit steps 1 and 2 and add the essence after straining the custard in step 6.
• If the custard is to be used cold, chill it quickly by placing the bowl in a larger container of iced water. Stir as the custard cools.
• For Liqueur Custard, add 30–45 ml/ 2–3 tbsp brandy, Kirsch or orange-flavour liqueur to the custard.

# Home-made Ice Cream

The simplest way to make home-made ice cream is to churn cold rich custard. Flavourings such as chocolate, fruit purée or liqueur can be added.

**1** Make a rich custard, using single cream or a mixture of milk and cream and following the instructions opposite. Strain and cool quickly.

**2** Pour the mixture into an ice-cream maker and freeze according to the manufacturer's instructions. Serve when ready, or freeze until required.

**3** Alternatively, freeze the mixture in a shallow freezerproof container until set, then chop into blocks and process in a food processor until smooth. Return to the freezer container. Repeat the process two or three times before finally freezing solid.

## COOK'S TIP

Remove home-made ice cream from the freezer about 20 minutes before serving and allow it to soften at room temperature.

# Raspberry Purée

A berry purée makes a vibrant sauce for a special pudding. Puddle some on a plate as a basis for a slice of rich gâteau.

**1** Place fresh hulled raspberries in a blender or food processor. Pulse the machine a few times, scraping down the bowl occasionally, until all the berries are puréed.

**2** If the berries are frozen, place them in a saucepan with a little sugar and soften over a gentle heat to release the juices. Simmer for 5 minutes, then cool.

**3** Press the purée through a fine-mesh nylon sieve to remove any fibres or seeds. Add icing sugar and either lemon juice or a fruit-flavour liqueur, to taste.

## Queen of Puddings

This pudding was developed from a seventeenth-century recipe by Queen Victoria's chefs and named in honour of the monarch.

*Serves 4*

INGREDIENTS
butter, for greasing
75 g/3 oz/1½ cups fresh
    breadcrumbs
60 ml/4 tbsp caster sugar, plus
    5 ml/1 tsp for the topping
grated rind of 1 lemon
600 ml/1 pint/2½ cups milk
4 eggs
45 ml/3 tbsp raspberry jam, warmed

*fresh breadcrumbs*

*caster sugar*

*grated lemon rind*

*milk*

*eggs*

*raspberry jam*

**1** Grease a baking dish with butter. Stir the breadcrumbs, 30 ml/2 tbsp of the sugar and the lemon rind together in a bowl. Bring the milk to the boil in a pan, then stir into the breadcrumb mixture.

**2** Separate three of the eggs and beat the yolks with the whole egg. Stir into the breadcrumb mixture, pour into the baking dish and leave to stand for 30 minutes. Meanwhile, preheat the oven to 160°C/325°F/Gas 3. Bake the pudding for 50–60 minutes, until set.

### COOK'S TIP

The traditional recipe calls for raspberry jam, but the pudding is equally good with apricot preserve, lemon curd, marmalade or fruit purée.

**3** Whisk the egg whites in a large, grease-free bowl until stiff but not dry, then gradually whisk in the remaining 30 ml/2 tbsp caster sugar until the mixture is thick and glossy.

**4** Remove the pudding from the oven and spread the jam over the surface. Spoon over the meringue to cover the top completely. Sprinkle the extra sugar over the meringue, then bake for 15 minutes more, until the meringue is beginning to turn a light golden colour. Serve at once.

# Castle Puddings with Real Custard

Each of these individual puddings is crowned with jam and served with creamy custard.

*Serves 4*

INGREDIENTS
115 g/4 oz/½ cup butter, plus extra
    for greasing
about 90 ml/6 tbsp strawberry,
    blackcurrant or raspberry jam
115 g/4 oz/½ cup caster sugar
2 eggs, beaten
few drops of vanilla essence
130 g/3½ oz/generous 1 cup self-
    raising flour
herb sprigs, to decorate

FOR THE CUSTARD
4 eggs
15–30 ml/1–2 tbsp caster sugar
475 ml/16 fl oz/2 cups creamy milk
few drops of vanilla essence

butter

strawberry jam

caster sugar

eggs

vanilla essence

self-raising flour

milk

**1** Preheat the oven to 180°C/350°F/ Gas 4. Butter eight dariole moulds. Put about 10 ml/2 tsp jam in the base of each mould.

**4** Remove the moulds from the oven, leave to stand for a few minutes, then turn the puddings on to warmed plates. Decorate with herb sprigs and serve with the custard.

**2** Beat the butter and sugar until light and fluffy, then gradually beat in the eggs, beating well after each addition and adding the vanilla essence towards the end. Lightly fold in the flour, then divide the mixture among the moulds. Support the moulds on a baking sheet using crumpled foil and bake the puddings for 20 minutes or until a light golden colour.

**3** Meanwhile, make the custard. Whisk the eggs and sugar together. Bring the milk to the boil in a heavy-based pan, then slowly pour it on to the egg mixture, stirring. Return the mixture to the pan, add the vanilla essence and heat gently, stirring until the mixture thickens; do not allow it to boil. Cover the pan and remove it from the heat.

## COOK'S TIP
Instead of baking the puddings, you can steam them for 30–40 minutes. If you do not have dariole moulds, use ramekins.

# Baked Rice Pudding

Tender and creamy, this is one of the simplest
sweets, popular with people of all ages.

## Serves 4

INGREDIENTS
50 g/2 oz/4 tbsp butter, diced, plus
    extra for greasing
50 g/2 oz/¼ cup short-grain
    (pudding) rice
30 ml/2 tbsp soft light brown sugar
900 ml/1½ pints/3¾ cups milk
small strip of lemon rind
freshly grated nutmeg
herb sprigs, to decorate
hulled raspberries, to serve
    (optional)

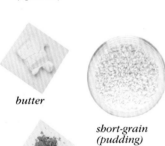

*butter*

*short-grain
(pudding)
rice*

*soft light
brown
sugar*

*milk*

*lemon*

*grated
nutmeg*

**1** Preheat the oven to 150°C/300°F/
Gas 2. Grease a 1.2 litre/2 pint/5 cup
shallow baking dish with a little butter.
Put the rice, sugar and butter into the
dish. Stir in the milk and lemon rind.

**2** Sprinkle a little nutmeg over the
surface. Bake the rice pudding for
30 minutes.

**3** Stir the rice pudding well, then
return it to the oven and bake for about
2 hours more, stirring until the rice is
tender and the pudding has a thick and
creamy consistency.

**4** If you like skin on top, leave the rice
pudding undisturbed for the final 30
minutes of cooking (otherwise, stir it
again). Serve hot, with hulled raspberries,
if you like. Decorate with herb sprigs.

## VARIATION

Baked rice pudding is delicious with
fruit. Instead of serving it with fresh
raspberries, choose sliced fresh
peaches or nectarines, strawberries
or lightly poached prunes. If you
prefer to add the fruit before
cooking, stir in sultanas, raisins or
chopped ready-to-eat dried apricots.

# Chocolate, Date and Walnut Pudding

Chocolate sponge with a gloriously gooey topping of date and nut is delicious on its own or with single cream.

## Serves 4

INGREDIENTS

25 g/1 oz/¼ cup chopped walnuts
25 g/1 oz/3 tbsp chopped dates
2 eggs, separated
5 ml/1 tsp vanilla essence
30 ml/2 tbsp golden caster sugar
45 ml/3 tbsp plain wholemeal flour
15 ml/1 tbsp cocoa powder
30 ml/2 tbsp milk

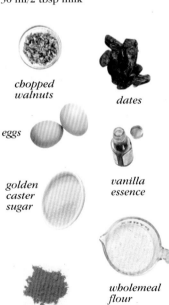

chopped walnuts

dates

eggs

golden caster sugar

vanilla essence

wholemeal flour

cocoa powder

milk

**1** Preheat the oven to 180°C/350°F/ Gas 4. Grease a 1.2 litre/2 pint/5 cup pudding basin and place a small circle of greaseproof or non-stick baking paper in the base. Mix together the walnuts and dates and spoon into the basin.

**2** Place the egg yolks in a heatproof bowl. Add the vanilla essence and sugar. Place the bowl over a pan of hot water and whisk until the mixture is thick and pale – a hand-held electric mixer makes the job easier.

**3** Sift the flour and cocoa into the mixture and fold them in with a metal spoon. Stir in the milk, to soften the mixture slightly. In a grease-free bowl, whisk the egg whites until they hold soft peaks; fold them in.

**4** Spoon the mixture into the basin and bake for 40–45 minutes, or until the pudding is well risen and firm to the touch. Run a knife around the pudding to loosen it from the basin, then turn it out and serve straight away.

# Baked Apple Dumplings

Baked apples dressed up to delight diners. The maple syrup sauce is the perfect accompaniment.

*Serves 8*

INGREDIENTS
475 g/1 lb 2 oz/4½ cups plain flour
2.5 ml/½ tsp salt
350 g/12 oz/1½ cups butter, plus extra for greasing
175–250 ml/6–8 fl oz/¾–1 cup iced water
8 firm cooking apples
1 egg white
150 g/5 oz/⅔ cup caster sugar
45 ml/3 tbsp whipping cream
2.5 ml/½ tsp vanilla essence
250 ml/8 fl oz/1 cup maple syrup
whipped cream, to serve

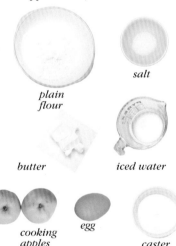

*plain flour*  *salt*  *butter*  *iced water*

*cooking apples*  *egg*  *caster sugar*  *vanilla essence*  *whipping cream*  *maple syrup*

**1** Sift the flour and salt into a large bowl. Rub in the butter until the mixture resembles breadcrumbs. Sprinkle with about 175 ml/6 fl oz/¾ cup iced water and mix to a dough. Gather into a ball. Wrap the dough in clear film and chill for at least 20 minutes. Preheat the oven to 220°C/425°F/Gas 7.

**2** Peel the apples, then remove the cores, cutting from the stem end, without cutting through the base. Roll out the pastry thinly. Cut squares almost large enough to enclose the apples, then brush these with egg white. Set an apple in the centre of each pastry square.

## COOK'S TIP

The easiest way to enclose the apples neatly is to pull up the points of the pastry squares around them, moistening the edges where they overlap. Mould the pastry around the apples, pleating the top neatly.

**3** Mix the sugar, cream and vanilla essence in a small bowl. Spoon into the hollow of each apple, then wrap each apple in pastry (see Cook's Tip), leaving the filled hollows exposed. Crimp the edges to seal, if you like.

**4** Set the apples in a large greased baking dish, at least 2 cm/¾ in apart. Bake for 30 minutes, then lower the temperature to 180°C/350°F/Gas 4 and continue baking for 20 minutes more, until the pastry is golden brown and the apples are tender.

**5** Transfer the dumplings to a serving dish. Mix the maple syrup with the juices in the baking dish and drizzle over the dumplings. Serve hot, accompanied by the whipped cream.

# Bread and Butter Pudding

An old favourite, but still immensely popular: the whisky sauce adds a touch of sophistication, but the pudding is equally good without it.

*Serves 4–6*

INGREDIENTS

50 g/2 oz/4 tbsp butter, melted, plus
    extra for greasing
4 ready-to-eat dried apricots, chopped
15 ml/1 tbsp raisins
30 ml/2 tbsp sultanas
15 ml/1 tbsp chopped mixed peel
1 French loaf (about 200 g/7 oz),
    thinly sliced
450 ml/¾ pint/scant 2 cups milk
150 ml/¼ pint/⅔ cup double cream
3 eggs
115 g/4 oz/½ cup caster sugar
2.5 ml/½ tsp vanilla essence

FOR THE WHISKY SAUCE
150 ml/¼ pint/⅔ cup double cream
30 ml/2 tbsp Greek-style yogurt
15 ml/1 tbsp caster sugar
15–30 ml/1–2 tbsp whisky

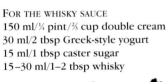

*butter*    *dried apricots*    *raisins*

*sultanas*    *chopped peel*

*milk*    *double cream*    *eggs*    *French loaf*

*caster sugar*

*Greek-style yogurt*    *vanilla essence*    *whisky*

**1** Lightly grease a deep 1.5 litre/ 2½ pint/6¼ cup ovenproof dish. Mix the dried fruits together and sprinkle a little of the mixture over the bottom of the dish. Brush both sides of the bread slices with melted butter. Layer the bread slices and dried fruit in the dish, finishing with a layer of bread.

**2** Heat the milk and cream together until just boiling. Meanwhile, whisk the eggs, sugar and vanilla essence in a bowl.

**3** Whisk the hot milk mixture into the eggs, then strain over the bread and fruit. Press the bread into the milk and egg mixture, cover with foil and leave to stand for 20 minutes. Preheat the oven to 180°C/350°F/Gas 4.

**4** Place the dish in a roasting tin half-filled with water and bake for about 1 hour or until the custard is just set. Remove the foil and bake the pudding for 10 minutes more, or until the bread is golden. Just before serving, make the sauce by heating the cream gently with the Greek yogurt, sugar and whisky. Stir frequently. Serve with the hot pudding.

# Sticky Toffee Pudding

This is one of those puddings everyone always has room for. The sponge is full of flavour and the sauce is irresistible.

*Serves 6*

INGREDIENTS
175 g/6 oz/¾ cup butter, plus extra
    for greasing
115 g/4 oz/1 cup toasted walnuts,
    chopped
175 g/6 oz/scant 1 cup soft light
    brown sugar
60 ml/4 tbsp double cream
30 ml/2 tbsp lemon juice
2 eggs, beaten
115 g/4 oz/1 cup self-raising flour
icing sugar, to dust

*butter*

*chopped
walnuts*

*soft light
brown sugar*

*double cream*

*lemon*

*eggs*

*self-raising
flour*

**1** Grease a 900 ml/1½ pint/3¾ cup pudding basin with butter and add half the nuts. Heat 50 g/2 oz/4 tbsp of the butter with 50 g/2 oz/4 tbsp of the sugar, the cream and 15 ml/1 tbsp of the lemon juice in a small pan, stirring until the mixture is smooth.

**2** Pour half the melted mixture into the pudding basin, then swirl to coat it a little way up the sides. Beat the remaining butter and sugar until light and fluffy, then gradually beat in the eggs. Fold in the flour and the remaining nuts and lemon juice and spoon into the pudding basin.

**3** Prepare a steamer. Cover the basin with greaseproof paper with a pleat folded in the centre, then tie securely with string. Steam the pudding for about 1¼ hours, until set in the centre.

**4** Just before serving, gently warm the remaining melted mixture. Turn out the pudding on a warm plate, dust with icing sugar, and pour over the warm sauce.

## COOK'S TIP

If you do not have a steamer, half-fill a large saucepan with water and bring it to the boil. Place an upturned saucer or trivet in the pan to support the pudding basin – the water should come about half-way up the sides of the basin. Cover with a tight-fitting lid.

# Chocolate Chip and Banana Pudding

Hot and steamy, this superb, light pudding has a beguiling banana and chocolate flavour.

### Serves 4

INGREDIENTS

75 g/3 oz/6 tbsp unsalted butter or
    margarine, plus extra for greasing
200 g/7oz/1¾ cups self-raising flour
2 ripe bananas
75 g/3 oz/⅓ cup caster sugar
60 ml/4 tbsp milk
1 egg, beaten
60 ml/4 tbsp plain chocolate chips

FOR THE CHOCOLATE SAUCE

115 g/4 oz/½ cup caster sugar
60 ml/4 tbsp water
175 g/6 oz plain chocolate, broken
    into squares
30 ml/2 tbsp unsalted butter
30 ml/2 tbsp brandy or orange juice

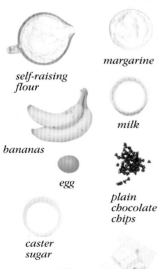

*self-raising flour*

*margarine*

*bananas*

*milk*

*egg*

*plain chocolate chips*

*caster sugar*

*butter*

*brandy*

**1** Prepare a steamer or half-fill a saucepan with water and bring it to the boil. Grease a 1 litre/1¾ pint/4 cup pudding basin. Sift the flour into a bowl and rub in the unsalted butter or margarine until the mixture resembles coarse breadcrumbs.

**2** Mash the bananas in a bowl. Stir them into the creamed mixture, with the caster sugar.

**3** Whisk the milk with the egg in a jug or bowl, then beat into the pudding mixture. Stir in the chocolate chips.

**4** Spoon the mixture into the prepared basin, cover closely with a double thickness of pleated foil, and steam for 2 hours, topping up the water as required during cooking.

**5** Make the sauce. Place the sugar and water in a saucepan and heat gently, stirring occasionally, until the sugar has dissolved. Stir in the chocolate, until melted, then add the butter. Do not allow the sauce to boil. Stir in the brandy or orange juice and keep warm.

**6** Run a knife around the top of the pudding to loosen it, then turn it out on to a serving dish. Serve hot, with the chocolate sauce.

### COOK'S TIP

If you have a food processor, make a quick-mix version by processing together all the ingredients, except the chocolate chips, until smooth. Stir in the chocolate and proceed as described in the recipe.

# Baked Blackberry Cheesecake

This light, low-fat cheesecake is best made with wild blackberries, if they are in season, but cultivated ones will do; or substitute other soft fruit, such as raspberries or blueberries.

*Serves 4–6*

INGREDIENTS
175 g/6 oz/¾ cup cottage cheese
150 g/5 oz/⅔ cup low-fat natural
    yogurt
15 ml/1 tbsp plain wholemeal flour
25 g/1 oz/2 tbsp golden caster sugar
1 egg, plus 1 egg white
finely grated rind and juice of
    ½ lemon
200 g/7 oz/2 cups fresh or frozen
    and thawed blackberries

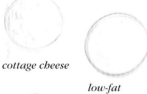
*cottage cheese*

*low-fat
natural yogurt*

*plain
wholemeal flour*

*golden caster
sugar*

*eggs*

*lemon*

*blackberries*

## COOK'S TIP
If you prefer to use canned blackberries, choose those canned in natural juice and drain the fruit well before adding it to the cheesecake mixture. The juice can be served with the cheesecake.

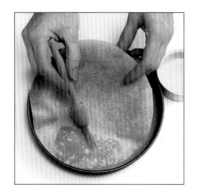

**1** Preheat the oven to 180°C/350°F/Gas 4. Lightly grease and base-line an 18 cm/7 in sandwich cake tin.

**2** Place the cottage cheese in a food processor and process until smooth. Alternatively, rub it through a sieve. Scrape the smooth mixture into a bowl.

**3** Stir in the yogurt, flour, sugar, egg and egg white. Fold in the lemon rind and juice and the blackberries, reserving a few for decoration.

**4** Tip the mixture into the prepared tin and level the surface. Bake for 30–35 minutes, or until the mixture is just set. Switch off the oven and leave for a further 30 minutes.

**5** Run a knife around the edge of the cheesecake, and then turn it out. Remove the lining paper and place the cheesecake on a warm serving plate.

**6** Decorate the cheesecake with the reserved blackberries. Serve warm.

# Apple Brown Betty

Crisp, spicy breadcrumbs layered with lemony apples make a simply delicious dessert.

## Serves 6

INGREDIENTS

50 g/2 oz/1 cup fresh white
    breadcrumbs
50 g/2 oz/4 tbsp butter, plus extra
    for greasing
175 g/6 oz/1 cup soft light
    brown sugar
2.5 ml/½ tsp ground cinnamon
1.5 ml/¼ tsp ground cloves
1.5 ml/¼ tsp grated nutmeg
900 g/2 lb cooking apples
juice of 1 lemon
25 g/1 oz/¼ cup finely chopped
    walnuts

*fresh white breadcrumbs*

*butter*

*soft light brown sugar*

*ground cinnamon*

*grated nutmeg*

*cooking apples*

*lemon*

*chopped walnuts*

**1** Preheat the grill. Spread out the breadcrumbs on a baking sheet or in a roasting tin and toast under the grill until golden, stirring frequently to colour them evenly. Set aside.

**2** Preheat the oven to 190°C/375°F/ Gas 5. Grease a large, deep ovenproof dish with a little butter. Mix the sugar with the spices. Cut the butter into tiny pieces, then set aside.

**3** Peel, core, and slice the apples. Toss immediately with the lemon juice to prevent them from turning brown.

**4** Sprinkle a thin layer of breadcrumbs into the dish. Cover with one-third of the apples and sprinkle with one-third of the sugar and spice mixture. Add another layer of breadcrumbs and dot with one-third of the butter. Repeat the layers twice more, sprinkling the nuts on top of the final layer of breadcrumbs before dotting the remaining butter over the surface.

**5** Bake for 35–40 minutes, until the apples are tender and the top is golden brown. Serve warm.

# Pear and Cherry Crunch

A triumph of contrasting textures and flavours, this pudding pairs fresh and dried fruit with a nut and crumb topping.

*Serves 6*

INGREDIENTS
115 g/4 oz/½ cup butter, plus extra
    for greasing
1 kg/2¼ lb pears, about 8
45 ml/3 tbsp lemon juice
175 g/6 oz/3 cups fresh
    white breadcrumbs
75 g/3 oz/⅔ cup dried cherries or
    stoned prunes, chopped
65 g/2½ oz/⅔ cup coarsely
    chopped hazelnuts
115 g/4 oz/⅔ cup soft light
    brown sugar
fresh mint sprigs, to decorate
whipped cream, to serve

*butter*

*pears*

*lemon*

*fresh white
breadcrumbs*

*prunes*

*hazelnuts*

*soft light
brown
sugar*

**1** Preheat the oven to 190°C/375°F/
Gas 5. Grease a 20 cm/8 in square cake
tin. Peel, core and chop the pears. Place
them in a bowl and sprinkle them with
the lemon juice to prevent them from
turning brown.

**2** Melt 75 g/3 oz/6 tbsp of the butter.
Stir in the breadcrumbs. Spread a scant
one-third of the crumb mixture on the
bottom of the prepared tin.

**3** Top with half the pears. Sprinkle
over half the dried cherries or prunes,
half the hazelnuts and half the sugar.
Repeat the layers, then sprinkle the
remaining crumbs over the surface.

**4** Dice the remaining butter and dot it
over the surface. Bake for 30–35
minutes, until golden. Serve hot, with
whipped cream. Decorate each portion
with a sprig of fresh mint.

# Apple Charlotte

This classic dessert takes its name from the straight-sided tin with heart-shaped handles in which it is traditionally baked. The buttery bread crust encases a sweet yet sharp apple purée.

*Serves 6*

INGREDIENTS

1.2 kg/2½ lb cooking apples
30 ml/2 tbsp water
115 g/4 oz/⅔ cup soft light
    brown sugar
2.5 ml/½ tsp ground cinnamon
1.5 ml/¼ tsp grated nutmeg
7 slices firm textured white bread
75 g/3 oz/6 tbsp butter, melted
custard, to serve (optional)

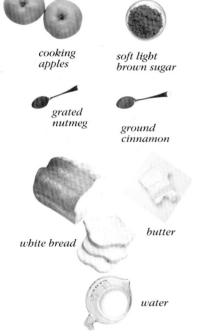

*cooking apples*

*soft light brown sugar*

*grated nutmeg*

*ground cinnamon*

*white bread*

*butter*

*water*

**1** Peel, quarter and core the apples. Cut them into thick slices and put them into a large heavy-based saucepan with the water. Cover and cook over a medium-low heat for 5 minutes, then remove the lid and cook for 10 minutes, until the apples are very soft.

**2** Add the sugar and spices and continue cooking, stirring frequently, until the apples are soft and thick. (There should be about 750 ml/1¼ pints/3 cups of apple purée.)

**3** Preheat the oven to 200°C/400°F/ Gas 6. Trim the crusts from the bread and brush with melted butter on one side. Cut two slices into triangles and use as many as necessary to cover the base of a 1.5 litre/2½ pint/6¼ cup charlotte tin or soufflé dish, placing them buttered-side down and fitting them in tightly. Cut fingers of bread the same height as the tin or dish and use them to line the sides completely, overlapping them slightly.

**4** Spoon the apple purée into the tin or dish. Cover the top with bread slices, buttered-side up, cutting them as necessary to fit. Bake for 20 minutes, then reduce the oven temperature to 180°C/350°F/Gas 4 and bake for 25 minutes, until well browned and firm. Leave to stand for 15 minutes, then turn out on to a serving plate. Serve with custard, if you like.

## COOK'S TIP

If preferred, microwave the apple slices without water in a large glass dish at high (100% power), tightly covered, for 15 minutes. Add the sugar and spices and microwave, uncovered, for a further 15 minutes, until very thick, stirring occasionally.

# PIES, CRUMBLES & TARTS

## Lemon Meringue Pie

A good lemon meringue pie combines crisp pastry with a tart filling topped with melt-in-the-mouth meringue: a perennial favourite.

*Serves 8*

INGREDIENTS
115 g/4 oz/1 cup plain flour
2.5 ml/½ tsp salt
65 g/2½ oz/5 tbsp butter, diced
30 ml/2 tbsp iced water

FOR THE FILLING
grated rind and juice of 1
    large lemon
250 ml/8 fl oz/1 cup cold water
200 g/7 oz/scant 1 cup
    granulated sugar
25 g/1 oz/2 tbsp butter
45 ml/3 tbsp cornflour mixed with
    15 ml/1 tbsp water
3 eggs, separated
pinch of salt
pinch of cream of tartar

*plain flour*

*salt*

*butter*

*lemon*

*granulated sugar*

*cornflour*

*eggs*

*cream of tartar*

**1** Sift the flour and salt into a bowl. Rub in the butter until the mixture resembles breadcrumbs, then stir in just enough water to bind the dough. Roll it out on a lightly floured surface and line a 23 cm/9 in pie plate, trimming the edge to leave a 1 cm/½ in overhang.

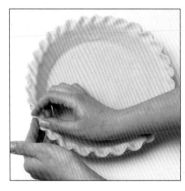

**2** Fold the overhang under and crimp the edge. Chill the pastry case for at least 20 minutes. Meanwhile, preheat the oven to 200°C/400°F/Gas 6.

**3** Prick the dough all over with a fork. Line with crumpled foil. Bake for 12 minutes, then remove the foil. Continue baking for 6–8 minutes more, or until golden.

**4** Make the filling. Heat the lemon rind and juice with the water, 115 g/4 oz/ ½ cup of the sugar, and the butter. Combine the cornflour mixture with the egg yolks. When the lemon mixture boils, stir in the cornflour mixture, whisking until the mixture thickens. Cover the surface with greaseproof paper.

**5** Make the meringue by beating the egg whites in a grease-free bowl with the salt and cream of tartar until they hold stiff peaks. Add the remaining sugar and beat until glossy.

**6** Spoon the lemon mixture into the pastry case and spread level. Spoon the meringue on top, smoothing it up to the edge of the crust to seal. Bake for 12–15 minutes, until the meringue is tinged with gold.

# Cider Pie

Versions of this old-fashioned pie are to be found on both sides of the Atlantic. Reducing the cider intensifies the flavour.

## Serves 6

INGREDIENTS
175 g/6 oz/1½ cups plain flour
1.5 ml/¼ tsp salt
10 ml/2 tsp granulated sugar
115 g/4 oz/½ cup cold butter
about 60 ml/4 tbsp iced water

FOR THE FILLING
600 ml/1 pint/2½ cups cider
15 g/½ oz/1 tbsp butter
250 ml/8 fl oz/1 cup maple syrup
60 ml/4 tbsp water
2 eggs, separated
5 ml/1 tsp grated nutmeg

plain
flour

salt

granulated
sugar

butter

maple syrup

cider

eggs

grated
nutmeg

**1** Sift the flour and salt into a bowl. Add the sugar. Using a pastry blender, cut in the butter until the mixture resembles breadcrumbs. Add enough iced water to bind the dough. Gather it into a ball, place in a polythene bag and chill for at least 20 minutes.

**2** Meanwhile, for the filling, place the cider in a saucepan and boil until only 175 ml/6 fl oz/¾ cup remains, then cool.

**3** Roll out the pastry thinly between two sheets of greaseproof paper or non-stick baking paper. Line a 23 cm/9 in pie dish with the pastry.

**4** Trim the edge of the pastry case, leaving a 1 cm/½ in overhang. Fold the overhang under to form the edge. Using a fork, press the edge to the rim of the dish and push up from underneath with your fingers to create a ruffle effect. Chill the pastry case for at least 20 minutes. Preheat the oven to 180°C/350°F/ Gas 4.

**5** For the filling, add the butter, maple syrup and water to the cider. Simmer gently for 5–6 minutes. Remove the pan from the heat and leave the mixture to cool slightly, then whisk in the beaten egg yolks.

**6** Whisk the egg whites in a large, grease-free bowl until they form stiff peaks. Fold in the cider mixture gently until evenly blended.

**7** Pour the mixture into the prepared pastry case. Dust with the grated nutmeg. Bake the pie for 30–35 minutes, until the pastry is golden brown and the filling has set. Serve warm.

# Mississippi Pecan Pie

An American favourite, pecan pie is now universally popular.

*Serves 6–8*

INGREDIENTS
115 g/4 oz/1 cup plain flour
50 g/2 oz/4 tbsp butter, cubed
25 g/1 oz/2 tbsp caster sugar
1 egg yolk
about 30 ml/2 tbsp cold water
cream or ice cream, to serve

FOR THE FILLING
175 g/6 oz/½ cup golden syrup
50 g/2 oz/⅓ cup dark
    muscovado sugar
50 g/2 oz/4 tbsp butter
3 eggs, lightly beaten
2.5 ml/½ tsp vanilla essence
150 g/5 oz/1¼ cups pecan nuts

plain
flour

butter

caster
sugar

eggs

golden
syrup

muscovado sugar

vanilla
essence

pecan
nuts

## COOK'S TIP

The filling may look a little soft when the pie is removed from the oven, but it will rapidly firm up as the pie cools slightly.

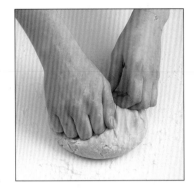

**1** Place the flour in a bowl. Rub in the butter until the mixture resembles breadcrumbs, then stir in the sugar, egg yolk and enough water to bind the dough. Knead lightly on a floured surface until smooth.

**2** Roll out the pastry and line a 20 cm/ 8 in loose-based fluted flan tin. Prick the base, then line with greaseproof paper and fill with baking beans. Chill for 30 minutes. Preheat the oven to 200°C/ 400°F/Gas 6.

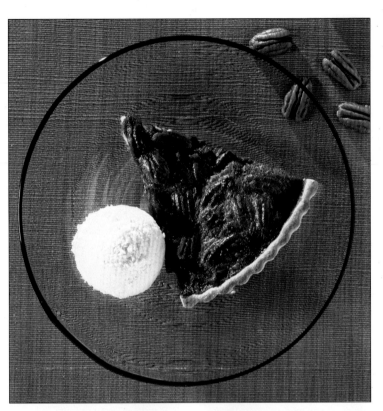

**3** Bake the pastry case for 10 minutes. Lift out the paper and beans and bake for 5 minutes more. Set aside to cool. Reduce the oven temperature to 180°C/350°F/Gas 4.

**4** Meanwhile, make the filling. Heat the syrup, sugar and butter in a pan until the sugar dissolves. Remove from the heat and cool slightly. Whisk in the eggs and vanilla essence and stir in the pecans. Pour into the pastry case and bake for 35–40 minutes, until the filling is set. Serve warm, with cream or ice cream.

# Apple Crumble Cake

This is a wonderful way of using windfall apples, and it makes a satisfying and tasty sweet for a cool autumn evening.

*Serves 8–10*

INGREDIENTS
50 g/2 oz/4 tbsp butter, softened,
    plus extra for greasing
75 g/3 oz/6 tbsp caster sugar
1 egg, beaten
115 g/4 oz/1 cup self-raising
    flour, sifted
2 cooking apples
50 g/2 oz/⅓ cup sultanas

FOR THE TOPPING
75 g/3 oz/¾ cup self-raising flour
2.5 ml/½ tsp ground cinnamon
40 g/1½ oz/3 tbsp butter
25 g/1 oz/2 tbsp caster sugar

FOR THE DECORATION
1 red dessert apple, cored, thinly
    sliced and tossed in lemon juice
30 ml/2 tbsp caster sugar
ground cinnamon, for sprinkling

*butter*    *caster sugar*    *egg*

*self-raising flour*    *cooking apples*

*sultanas*    *ground cinnamon*

**1** Preheat the oven to 180°C/350°F/Gas 4. Grease and base-line a deep 18 cm/7 in springform tin. Make the topping. Sift the flour and cinnamon into a mixing bowl. Rub in the butter until the mixture resembles breadcrumbs, then stir in the sugar. Set aside.

**2** Put the butter, sugar, egg and flour into a bowl and beat for 1–2 minutes until smooth. Spoon the mixture into the prepared tin.

**3** Peel, core and slice the cooking apples into a bowl. Add the sultanas. Spread the mixture evenly over the cake mixture, then sprinkle with the crumble topping. Bake for about 1 hour.

**4** Allow to cool in the tin for 10 minutes before turning out on to a wire rack and peeling off the lining paper. Serve warm or cool, decorated with slices of red dessert apple with a sprinkling of caster sugar and cinnamon.

## COOK'S TIP
This cake can be kept for up to 2 days in an airtight container.

# Chocolate Lemon Tartlets

Pastry tartlets can be prepared a day ahead, but they are best filled just a few hours before serving so that the fillings are still soft.

*Makes 12*

INGREDIENTS
200 g/7 oz shortcrust pastry, thawed
   if frozen
melted chocolate and lemon peel
   twists, to decorate

FOR THE LEMON CUSTARD SAUCE
grated rind and juice of 1 lemon
350 ml/12 fl oz/1½ cups milk
6 egg yolks
50 g/2 oz/¼ cup caster sugar

FOR THE LEMON CURD FILLING
grated rind and juice of 2 lemons
175 g/6 oz/¾ cup butter, diced
450 g/1 lb/2 cups granulated sugar
3 eggs, lightly beaten

FOR THE CHOCOLATE LAYER
175 g/6 oz dark or plain chocolate,
   chopped
175 ml/6 fl oz/¾ cup double cream
25 g/1 oz/2 tbsp butter, diced

**1** Make the custard sauce. Mix the lemon rind and milk in a saucepan. Bring to the boil, then remove from the heat and set aside for 5 minutes to infuse. Reheat the milk gently. Beat the egg yolks and sugar until pale and thick. Pour over about 250 ml/8 fl oz/1 cup of the hot milk, beating vigorously. Return the yolk mixture to the pan and cook gently, stirring until the mixture thickens and lightly coats the back of a spoon. Strain into a chilled bowl and stir in the lemon juice. Cool, stirring occasionally, then chill until needed.

**2** Make the lemon curd filling. Combine the lemon rind, juice, butter and sugar in the top of a double boiler. Heat over simmering water until the butter has melted and the sugar dissolved. Reduce the heat to low. Stir in the eggs. Cook over a low heat, stirring constantly, until the mixture thickens and coats the back of a spoon. Strain into a bowl and cover the surface with clear film. Cool, stirring occasionally, then chill until thick, continuing to stir occasionally.

**3** Lightly butter twelve 7.5 cm/3 in tartlet tins. Roll out the pastry and cut out twelve 10 cm/4 in rounds. Press each one into a tartlet tin. Prick the base. Place the tins on a baking sheet and chill for 30 minutes. Preheat the oven to 190°C/375°F/Gas 5. Line the tartlet cases with crumpled foil; bake blind for 5–8 minutes. Remove the foil and bake for 5 more minutes, until golden brown. Cool on a wire rack.

*shortcrust pastry*

*plain chocolate*

*lemon*

*milk*

*eggs*

*caster sugar*

*butter*

*granulated sugar*

*double cream*

## COOK'S TIP
Instead of individual tartlets you could make one large tart, using a loose-based flan tin of 20 cm/8 in diameter, placed on a baking sheet. Bake the pastry case as for the tartlets, but for a total of 20–25 minutes or until golden brown.

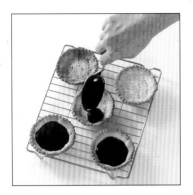

**4** Prepare the chocolate layer. Melt the chocolate with the cream over a low heat. Beat in the butter and cool slightly. Pour the chocolate filling into each tartlet to make a layer of 5 mm/¼ in thick. Chill for 10 minutes until set. Remove the tartlets from the tins and spoon in a layer of lemon curd. Set aside, but do not chill or the chocolate layer will be too firm. Spoon a little custard on to a plate and place a tartlet in the centre. Decorate with a lemon peel twist and drops of melted chocolate feathered with a skewer.

# Banoffee Pie

Any combination of caramel toffee and banana is bound to be a winner. This is one of those 'new traditional' puddings that is going to be around for a long time.

*Serves 6–8*

INGREDIENTS
150 g/5 oz/1¼ cups plain flour
225 g/8 oz/1 cup butter
50 g/2 oz/4 tbsp caster sugar
½ x 400 g/14 oz can skimmed,
    sweetened condensed milk
115 g/4 oz/⅔ cup soft light
    brown sugar
30 ml/2 tbsp golden syrup
2 small bananas, sliced
a little lemon juice
whipped cream and 5 ml/1 tsp
    grated plain chocolate,
    to decorate

*plain flour*

*butter*

*caster sugar*

*condensed milk*

*soft light brown sugar*

*golden syrup*

*bananas*

*lemon*

*whipping cream*

*plain chocolate*

**1** Preheat the oven to 160°C/325°F/Gas 3. Place the flour and half the butter in a food processor and blend until crumbled (or rub in with your fingertips). Stir in the caster sugar. Squeeze the mixture together to form a dough.

**2** Press the dough into the base of a 20 cm/8 in loose-based fluted flan tin. Bake for 25–30 minutes, until the dough is lightly browned.

**3** Heat the remaining butter with the condensed milk, brown sugar and golden syrup in a non-stick saucepan. Stir until the butter has melted and the sugar dissolved, then cook for 7 minutes, stirring constantly, until the mixture thickens and turns a pale caramel colour. Pour on to the cooked pastry base and leave until cold.

**4** Sprinkle the bananas with lemon juice and arrange in overlapping circles on top of the caramel filling, leaving a gap in the centre. Fill the banana ring with swirls of whipped cream and sprinkle with the grated chocolate.

# Bakewell Tart

Although the pastry base makes this a tart, it was originally known as Bakewell pudding.

*Serves 4*

INGREDIENTS
225 g/8 oz puff pastry, thawed
   if frozen
30 ml/2 tbsp raspberry or
   apricot jam
2 eggs, plus 2 egg yolks
115 g/4 oz/½ cup caster sugar
115 g/4 oz/½ cup butter, melted
50 g/2 oz/⅔ cup ground almonds
few drops of almond essence
icing sugar, for dusting

 *puff pastry*  *raspberry jam*

 *eggs* *caster sugar*

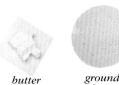 *butter* *ground almonds*

 *almond essence*

**1** Preheat the oven to 200°C/400°F/ Gas 6. Roll out the pastry on a lightly floured surface and use it to line an 18 cm/7 in pie plate or loose-based flan tin. Spread the jam over the bottom of the pastry case.

**2** Whisk the whole eggs, egg yolks and caster sugar in a large bowl until thick and pale, then gently stir in the melted butter, ground almonds and almond essence.

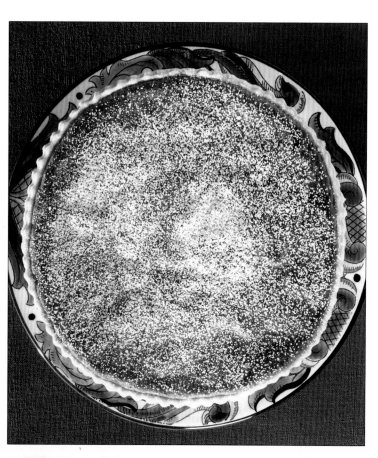

**3** Pour the mixture into the pastry case and bake for 30 minutes, until the filling is just set and browned. Sift icing sugar over the top before serving hot, warm or cold.

## COOK'S TIP

As this pastry case is not baked blind before it is filled, it is a good idea to place the flan tin on a hot baking sheet for baking to ensure that the bottom of the pastry case cooks right through. Simply place the baking sheet in the oven when you switch it on to preheat.

# Jam Tart

The Queen of Hearts knew a thing or two when she expressed a preference for jam tarts. Small or large, they are traditional treats.

*Serves 6–8*

INGREDIENTS
200 g/7 oz/1¾ cups plain flour
pinch of salt
50 g/2 oz/¼ cup granulated sugar
115 g/4 oz/½ cup butter, chilled
1 egg
1.5 ml/¼ tsp grated lemon rind
350 g/12 oz/1¼ cups fruit jam, such
    as strawberry, raspberry, or apricot

FOR THE GLAZE
1 egg
30 ml/2 tbsp whipping cream

*plain flour*

*salt*

*granulated sugar*

*butter*

*eggs*

*grated lemon rind*

*strawberry jam*

*whipping cream*

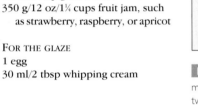

**1** Place the flour, salt and sugar in a mixing bowl. Using a pastry blender or two knives, cut in the butter until the mixture resembles breadcrumbs. Beat the egg with the lemon rind, then pour it over the flour mixture and mix to a dough. Mix in 15–30 ml/1–2 tbsp of water if necessary.

**2** Gather the dough into two balls, one slightly larger than the other, and flatten into discs. Wrap in greaseproof paper, and chill for at least 40 minutes, then roll out the larger ball of dough on a floured surface and line a 23 cm/9 in loose-based tart tin.

**3** Preheat the oven to 190°C/375°F/ Gas 5. Spread the jam evenly over the bottom of the pastry case. Roll out the remaining pastry and cut it into strips about 1 cm/½ in wide.

**4** Arrange the pastry strips over the jam in a lattice pattern. Trim the edges of the strips even with the edge of the tin, pressing them lightly on to the pastry case. Make the glaze by beating the egg with the cream. Brush the mixture over the pastry. Bake for about 35 minutes, or until the crust is golden brown. Allow to cool before serving.

# Peanut Butter Tart

This sumptuously creamy tart in a crunchy biscuit crust will delight fans of peanut butter.

*Serves 8*

INGREDIENTS

75 g/3 oz/6 tbsp butter, melted, plus extra for greasing
175 g/6 oz digestive biscuits, crushed
50 g/2 oz/⅓ cup soft light brown sugar
whipped cream or ice cream, to serve

FOR THE FILLING

3 egg yolks
115 g/4 oz/½ cup caster sugar
50 g/2 oz/⅓ cup soft light brown sugar
25 g/1 oz/¼ cup cornflour
600 ml/1 pint/2½ cups evaporated milk
25 g/1 oz/2 tbsp butter, diced
7.5 ml/1½ tsp vanilla essence
115 g/4 oz/⅓ cup crunchy peanut butter
75 g/3 oz/¾ cup icing sugar

*digestive biscuits*

*soft light brown sugar*

*butter*

*eggs*

*caster sugar*

*cornflour*

*vanilla essence*

*evaporated milk*

*crunchy peanut butter*

*icing sugar*

**1** Preheat the oven to 180°C/350°F/Gas 4. Grease a 23 cm/9in pie dish. Mix the biscuit crumbs, sugar and melted butter in a bowl. Spread the mixture in the prepared dish and press it down evenly over the base and sides. Bake for 10 minutes, then remove from the oven and cool. Leave the oven on.

**2** Make the filling. Mix the egg yolks, sugars and cornflour in a heavy-based saucepan. Slowly whisk in the evaporated milk, then cook over a medium heat for 8–10 minutes, stirring constantly, until the mixture thickens. Reduce the heat to very low and cook for 3–4 minutes more, until very thick.

**3** Beat in the butter and vanilla essence. Remove the pan from the heat, cover the surface closely with clear film and cool.

**4** Combine the peanut butter and icing sugar in a small bowl, working with your fingertips to blend the ingredients to the consistency of fine breadcrumbs.

**5** Sprinkle all but 45 ml/3 tbsp of the peanut butter crumbs evenly over the base of the crumb crust.

**6** Pour in the filling, spreading it evenly, then sprinkle with the remaining crumbs. Bake for 15 minutes. Leave the pie to cool for at least 1 hour. Serve with whipped cream or ice cream.

# Rich Chocolate-berry Tart

Raspberries, blackberries, alpine strawberries or loganberries, or a combination, can be used to top this tart.

*Serves 10*

INGREDIENTS
115 g/4 oz/½ cup butter, softened,
    plus extra for greasing
115 g/4 oz/½ cup caster sugar
2.5 ml/½ tsp salt
15 ml/1 tbsp vanilla essence
50 g/2 oz/½ cup cocoa powder
175 g/6 oz/1½ cups plain flour
450 g/1 lb fresh berries, for topping

FOR THE GANACHE FILLING
475 ml/16 fl oz/2 cups double cream
150 g/5 oz/½ cup seedless
    blackberry or raspberry preserve
225 g/8 oz dark chocolate, chopped
25 g/1 oz/2 tbsp butter, diced

FOR THE BERRY SAUCE
225 g/8 oz fresh or frozen
    blackberries or raspberries
15 ml/1 tbsp lemon juice
25 g/1 oz/2 tbsp caster sugar
30 ml/2 tbsp seedless blackberry or
    raspberry preserve

**1** Make the pastry. In a food processor, process the butter, sugar, salt and vanilla essence until creamy. Add the cocoa and process for 1 minute, then scrape down the sides of the bowl. Add the flour all at once and pulse until just blended. Place a piece of clear film on the work surface. Turn out the dough on to the clear film. Use the clear film to help shape the dough into a flat disc; wrap tightly. Chill for 1 hour.

**2** Lightly grease a 23 cm/9 in loose-based tart tin. Let the dough soften slightly, then roll it out between sheets of clear film to a 28 cm/11 in round. Peel off the top sheet of the film and invert the dough into the tin. Ease the dough into the tin and lift off the remaining film. Neaten the pastry case.

**3** Prick the base of the pastry with a fork. Chill for 1 hour. Preheat the oven to 180°C/350°F/Gas 4. Line the pastry case with crumpled foil. Bake for 10 minutes, then remove the foil and bake for 5 minutes more, until just set. Remove to a wire rack to cool completely.

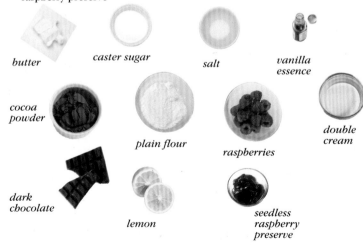

*butter*    *caster sugar*    *salt*    *vanilla essence*

*cocoa powder*    *plain flour*    *raspberries*    *double cream*

*dark chocolate*    *lemon*    *seedless raspberry preserve*

**4** Prepare the ganache filling. In a medium saucepan, bring the cream and blackberry or raspberry preserve to the boil. Remove from the heat and add the chocolate all at once, stirring until melted and smooth. Stir in the butter and strain into the cooled pastry case, smoothing level. Cool the tart completely.

## COOK'S TIP

If the chocolate pastry is too soft to roll, place it in the tin and press it over the bottom and up the sides. Don't be alarmed if the pastry case looks underdone when you remove it from the oven – it will dry out.

**5** Make the sauce. In a food processor combine the berries, lemon juice and sugar and process until smooth. Strain into a small bowl and add the preserve. If the sauce is too thick, add a little water.

**6** To serve, remove the tart from the tin. Place on a serving plate and arrange the berries on top. Brush the berries with a little of the sauce to glaze them. Serve the remaining sauce separately.

# COLD DESSERTS

# Cinnamon and Coconut Rice Pudding

Rice is a favourite pudding ingredient in many cuisines. This version introduces coconut milk and the warm flavour of cinnamon.

*Serves 4–6*

INGREDIENTS
40 g/1½ oz/¼ cup raisins
475 ml/16 fl oz/2 cups water, plus
　　extra for soaking the raisins
225 g/8 oz/1 cup short-grain
　　(pudding) rice
1 cinnamon stick
25 g/1 oz/2 tbsp caster sugar
475 ml/16 fl oz/2 cups milk
250 ml/8 fl oz/1 cup canned
　　sweetened coconut milk
2.5 ml/½ tsp vanilla essence
15 g/½ oz/1 tbsp butter, diced
25 g/1 oz/⅓ cup desiccated coconut
ground cinnamon, for sprinkling

**1** Place the raisins in a small bowl and pour over enough warm water to cover. Leave to soak.

**2** Bring the measured water to the boil in a medium-sized saucepan. Stir in the rice, cinnamon stick and sugar. Return to the boil, then lower the heat, cover and simmer gently for 15–20 minutes, until the liquid has been absorbed.

*raisins*

*short-grain (pudding) rice*

*cinnamon stick*

*caster sugar*

*milk*

*vanilla essence*

*butter*

*sweetened coconut milk*

*ground cinnamon*

*desiccated coconut*

**4** Preheat the grill. Tip the rice into a flameproof serving dish. Dot with the butter and sprinkle with the desiccated coconut. Grill about 13 cm/5 in from the heat for about 3–5 minutes, until the top is just browned. Sprinkle with cinnamon. Serve warm or cold.

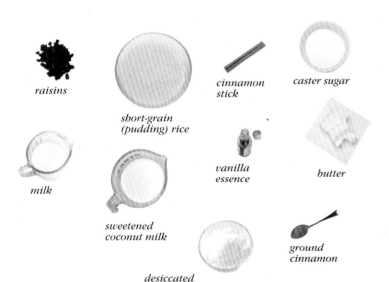

**3** Meanwhile, stir the milk, coconut milk and vanilla essence together in a bowl. Remove the cinnamon stick from the rice. Drain the raisins and stir them into the rice with the milk and coconut mixture. Cover and continue cooking, stirring often, for about 20 minutes, until the mixture is just thick but not mushy.

## COOK'S TIP
Always use pudding rice for milk puddings and rice desserts rather than other varieties. The short grains swell and absorb a great deal of liquid and cling together to produce a rich, creamy consistency.

# Sherry Trifle

Many versions of sherry trifle exist, but the traditional dessert takes a lot of beating.

## Serves 6–8

INGREDIENTS

175 g/6 oz trifle sponges, or
   2.5 cm/1 in cubes of plain
   Victoria sponge, or coarsely
   crumbled sponge fingers
60 ml/4 tbsp medium sherry
115 g/4 oz/⅓ cup raspberry jam
300 g/11 oz hulled raspberries
475 ml/16fl oz/2 cups custard,
   flavoured with 30 ml/2 tbsp
   medium or sweet sherry
300 ml/½ pint/1¼ cups sweetened
   whipped cream
toasted flaked almonds
mint leaves, to decorate

*sponge fingers*    *sherry*

*raspberry jam*    *raspberries*

*custard*

*flaked almonds*    *whipping cream*

## VARIATION

Use other ripe fruit in the trifle, with jam and liqueur to suit: try sliced apricots, peaches, nectarines or strawberries.

**1** Spread half the trifle sponges, cake cubes or sponge fingers over the bottom of a large glass serving bowl.

**2** Sprinkle half the sherry over the cake to moisten it. Spoon over half the jam, dotting it evenly over the cake.

**3** Reserve a few raspberries for decoration. Arrange half the remaining raspberries in a neat layer on top of the cake cubes.

**4** Pour over half the custard, covering the fruit and cake. Repeat the layers. Cover the trifle and chill for at least 2 hours.

**5** Before serving, spoon the sweetened whipped cream evenly over the trifle. Sprinkle with toasted flaked almonds and arrange the reserved raspberries and the mint leaves decoratively on the top.

# Ginger and Banana Brûlée

Desserts don't have to be elaborate to achieve excellent results. The proof of the pudding is this simple ginger and banana brûlée.

*Serves 6–8*

INGREDIENTS
4 thick slices ginger cake
6 bananas, sliced
30 ml/2 tbsp lemon juice
300 ml/½ pint/1¼ cups whipping
    cream or fromage frais
60 ml/4 tbsp fruit juice
30–45 ml/3–4 tbsp soft light
    brown sugar

*ginger cake*

*bananas*

*lemon*

*whipping cream*

*fruit juice*

*soft light brown sugar*

**1** Cut the cake into chunks and arrange in an ovenproof dish. Slice the bananas and toss in the lemon juice.

**2** Preheat the grill. Whip the cream until firm, then gently whip in the fruit juice. (If using fromage frais, just gently stir in the juice.) Drain the bananas and fold them into the mixture; spoon over the ginger cake.

**3** Sprinkle over the sugar in an even layer. Place under the hot grill for 2–3 minutes to caramelize. Serve at once, or allow to cool, then chill for a crisp topping.

## VARIATION
For a delicious alternative try chocolate cake and pears instead of ginger cake and bananas. You could also drizzle a little liqueur or sherry over the chocolate cake for a touch of luxury.

# White Chocolate Parfait

It's always party time when you serve this
spectacular creamy terrine, with its rich
chocolate coating.

*Serves 10*

INGREDIENTS
225 g/8 oz white chocolate,
  chopped
600 ml/1 pint/2½ cups whipping
  cream
120 ml/4 fl oz/½ cup milk
10 egg yolks
15 ml/1 tbsp caster sugar
25 g/1 oz/scant ½ cup desiccated
  coconut
120 ml/4 fl oz/½ cup canned
  sweetened coconut milk
150 g/5 oz/1¼ cups unsalted
  macadamia nuts
curls of fresh coconut, to decorate

FOR THE CHOCOLATE ICING
225 g/8 oz plain chocolate
75 g/3 oz/6 tbsp butter
20 ml/generous 1 tbsp golden syrup
175 ml/6 fl oz/¾ cup whipping
  cream

*white chocolate*

*whipping cream*

*milk*

*egg yolks*
*caster sugar*
*desiccated coconut*

*coconut milk*

*macadamia nuts*

*plain chocolate*
*butter*

**1** Using clear film, line the base and sides of a 1.5 litre/2½ pint/6¼ cup terrine or loaf tin, easing it into the corners and leaving a generous overlap.

**2** Place the white chocolate and 60 ml/4 tbsp of the cream in the top of a double boiler or in a heatproof bowl set over hot water. Stir until melted and smooth. Set aside.

**3** Put 250 ml/8 fl oz/1 cup of the cream in a pan. Add the milk and bring to the boil. Meanwhile, whisk the egg yolks and caster sugar together in a large bowl, until thick and pale.

**4** Add the hot cream mixture to the yolks, beating constantly. Pour back into the saucepan and cook over a low heat for 2–3 minutes, until thickened. Stir constantly and do not boil. Remove the pan from the heat, add the melted chocolate mixture, coconut and coconut milk, stir well and leave to cool.

**5** Whip the remaining cream until thick, then fold into the chocolate and coconut mixture. Pour about 475 ml/16 fl oz/2 cups of the parfait mixture into the prepared terrine or tin and spread evenly. Cover and freeze for about 2 hours, until just firm. Cover the remaining parfait mixture and chill.

**6** Scatter the macadamia nuts in an even layer over the parfait in the terrine or tin. Cover the nuts with the remaining parfait mixture. Cover the terrine and freeze for 6–8 hours or overnight, until the parfait is firm.

**7** Make the icing. Melt the chocolate with the butter and syrup in the top of a double boiler set over hot water. Stir occasionally. Meanwhile, heat the cream in a saucepan, until just simmering, then stir it into the chocolate mixture. Remove the pan from the heat and leave to cool until lukewarm.

**8** Turn out the terrine on to a rack placed over a baking sheet. Peel off the clear film, then pour the chocolate icing evenly over the top. Working quickly, smooth the icing down the sides with a palette knife. Leave to set slightly, then freeze for 3–4 hours more. Cut into slices using a knife dipped in hot water. Serve, decorated with coconut curls.

# Hazelnut Pavlova

Pavlova is an Australian invention, named after the ballerina Anna Pavlova and consisting of a light meringue base beneath a luscious cream and fruit topping.

## Serves 4–6

INGREDIENTS
3 egg whites
175 g/6 oz/¾ cup caster sugar
5 ml/1 tsp cornflour
5 ml/1 tsp white wine vinegar
40 g/1½ oz/5 tbsp chopped roasted
   hazelnuts
250 ml/8 fl oz/1 cup double cream
15 ml/1 tbsp orange juice
30 ml/2 tbsp natural thick and
   creamy yogurt
2 ripe nectarines, stoned and sliced
225 g/8 oz/2 cups hulled
   raspberries, halved
15–30 ml/1–2 tbsp redcurrant jelly,
   warmed

eggs

caster sugar

cornflour

white wine vinegar

hazelnuts

double cream

orange juice

yogurt

nectarines

raspberries

redcurrant jelly

**1** Preheat the oven to 140°C/275°F/ Gas 1. Lightly grease a baking sheet. Draw a 20 cm/8 in circle on a sheet of baking parchment. Place pencil-side down on the baking sheet.

**2** Place the egg whites in a clean, grease-free bowl and whisk until stiff. Whisk in the sugar, 15 ml/1 tbsp at a time, whisking well after each addition.

**3** Add the cornflour, vinegar and hazelnuts and fold in carefully with a large metal spoon. Spoon the meringue on to the marked circle and spread out to the edges, making a dip in the centre.

**4** Bake for 1¼–1½ hours, until crisp on the surface. Leave to cool completely and transfer to a serving platter. Whip the cream and orange juice until just thick, stir in the yogurt and spoon on to the meringue. Top with the fruit and drizzle over the redcurrant jelly. Serve immediately.

# Chocolate Tiramisu

This version of the famous Italian dessert substitutes a pastry case for the more conventional coffee-soaked biscuits.

*Serves 12–16*

INGREDIENTS

115 g/4 oz/½ cup butter, plus extra
    for greasing
15 ml/1 tbsp coffee-flavour liqueur
175 g/6 oz/1½ cups plain flour
25 g/1 oz/¼ cup cocoa powder, plus
    extra for dusting
25 g/1 oz/¼ cup icing sugar
pinch of salt
few drops of vanilla essence

FOR THE CHOCOLATE LAYER

120 ml/4 fl oz/½ cup double cream
15 ml/1 tbsp golden syrup
115 g/4 oz dark chocolate, chopped
25 g/1 oz/2 tbsp butter, diced
30 ml/2 tbsp coffee-flavour liqueur

FOR THE FILLING

250 ml/8 fl oz/1 cup double cream
350 g/12 oz/1½ cups
    mascarpone cheese
45 ml/3 tbsp icing sugar
45 ml/3 tbsp cold strong
    black coffee
45 ml/3 tbsp coffee-flavour liqueur
90 g/3½ oz plain chocolate, grated

*butter*

*plain flour*

*cocoa powder*

*icing sugar*

*vanilla essence*

*double cream*

*golden syrup*

*dark chocolate*

*mascarpone cheese*

*coffee-flavour liqueur*

**1** Lightly grease a 23 cm/9 in springform tin with butter. In a saucepan, melt the butter with the liqueur. Sift the flour, cocoa, sugar and salt into a bowl. Gradually stir in the vanilla essence and butter mixture until a soft dough forms. Knead lightly. Press on to the bottom and up the sides of the tin to within 2 cm/¾ in of the top. Prick the dough with a fork, then chill for 40 minutes.

**2** Preheat the oven to 190°C/375°F/ Gas 5. Bake the pastry case for 8–10 minutes. If the pastry puffs up, prick it with a fork and bake for 2–3 minutes more until set. Cool on a wire rack.

**3** Make the chocolate layer. Heat the cream and syrup. Allow to boil, then remove it from the heat and stir in the chocolate, until melted. Beat in the butter and liqueur and pour into the pastry case. Cool completely, then chill.

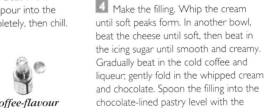

**4** Make the filling. Whip the cream until soft peaks form. In another bowl, beat the cheese until soft, then beat in the icing sugar until smooth and creamy. Gradually beat in the cold coffee and liqueur; gently fold in the whipped cream and chocolate. Spoon the filling into the chocolate-lined pastry level with the crust. Chill until ready to serve.

**5** To serve, run a sharp knife around the side of the tin to loosen the pastry. Unclip the tin side. Sift a layer of cocoa over the tart.

# Black Forest Sundae

There's more than one way to enjoy the classic Black Forest Gateau. Here the traditional ingredients are layered in a sundae glass to make a superb cold sweet.

## COOK'S TIP
Bottled black cherries often have a better flavour than canned ones, especially if the stones are left in. You needn't remove the stones – just remember to warn your guests.

## Serves 4

INGREDIENTS

400 g/14 oz can stoned black
   cherries in syrup
15 ml/1 tbsp cornflour
45 ml/3 tbsp Kirsch
150 ml/¼ pint/⅔ cup whipping
   cream
15 ml/1 tbsp icing sugar
600 ml/1 pint/2½ cups chocolate
   ice cream
115 g/4 oz chocolate cake
8 fresh cherries
vanilla ice cream, to serve

canned
black
cherries

cornflour

whipping
cream

chocolate
ice cream

chocolate
cake

fresh cherries

icing sugar

Kirsch

1 Strain the cherry syrup from the can into a saucepan. Spoon the cornflour into a small bowl and stir in 30 ml/2 tbsp of the strained cherry syrup.

2 Bring the syrup in the saucepan to the boil. Stir in the cornflour and syrup mixture. Simmer briefly, stirring, until the syrup thickens.

3 Add the drained canned cherries, stir in the Kirsch and spread on a metal tray to cool.

4 Whip the cream with the icing sugar.

5 Place a spoonful of the cherry mixture in the bottom of four sundae glasses. Continue with layers of ice cream, chocolate cake, whipped cream and more cherry mixture until the glasses are full.

6 Finish with a piece of chocolate cake, two scoops of ice cream and more cream. Decorate with the fresh cherries.

# Brown Bread Ice Cream

This dish sounds homely but tastes heavenly.
Toasted wholemeal breadcrumbs have a
wonderful nutty flavour, especially when
accentuated with hazelnuts.

## Serves 6

INGREDIENTS
50 g/2 oz/½ cup roasted and
   chopped hazelnuts, ground
75 g/3 oz/1½ cups fresh
   wholemeal breadcrumbs
50 g/2 oz/4 tbsp demerara sugar
3 egg whites
115 g/4 oz/½ cup caster sugar
300 ml/½ pint/1¼ cups double cream
few drops of vanilla essence
fresh mint sprigs, to decorate

FOR THE SAUCE
225 g/8 oz blackcurrants
75 g/3 oz/6 tbsp caster sugar
15 ml/1 tbsp crème de cassis

*hazelnuts*

*demerara sugar*  *fresh wholemeal breadcrumbs*

*eggs*  *caster sugar*

*double cream*  *vanilla essence*

*blackcurrants*  *crème de cassis*

**1** Preheat the grill. Combine the hazelnuts and breadcrumbs on a baking sheet, then sprinkle over the demerara sugar. Grill, stirring frequently, until the mixture is crisp and evenly browned. Leave to cool.

**2** Whisk the egg whites in a grease-free bowl until stiff, then gradually whisk in the caster sugar until thick and glossy. Whip the cream until it forms soft peaks and fold into the meringue with the breadcrumb mixture and vanilla essence.

**3** Spoon the mixture into a 1.2 litre/2 pint/5 cup loaf tin. Smooth the top level, then cover and freeze for several hours, or until firm.

**5** To serve, turn out the ice cream on to a plate and cut into slices. Arrange each slice on a serving plate, spoon over a little sauce and decorate with fresh mint sprigs.

**4** Meanwhile, make the sauce. Put the blackcurrants in a small bowl with the sugar. Toss gently to mix and leave for 30 minutes. Purée the blackcurrants in a blender or food processor, then press through a nylon sieve into a bowl. Stir in the crème de cassis and chill well.

## COOK'S TIP
To string blackcurrants, run a fork down the stalks so that the berries are pulled off by the tines.

# Chocolate Blancmange

As its name suggests, the blancmange was originally white, but the chocolate version is probably more popular today, especially when made with chocolate rather than cocoa powder.

*Serves 4*

INGREDIENTS
60 ml/4 tbsp cornflour
600 ml/1 pint/2½ cups milk
45 ml/3 tbsp granulated sugar
50–115 g/2–4 oz plain
    chocolate, chopped
few drops of vanilla essence
white and plain chocolate curls,
    to decorate

*cornflour*

*milk*

*granulated sugar*

*plain chocolate*

*vanilla essence*

*plain chocolate curls*

**1** Rinse a 750 ml/1¼ pint/3 cup fluted mould with cold water and leave it upside down to drain. Blend the cornflour to a smooth paste with a little of the milk.

**2** Bring the remaining milk to the boil, then pour on to the blended mixture, stirring all the time. Return all the milk to the saucepan and bring slowly to the boil, stirring until the mixture boils and thickens. Remove the pan from the heat, add the sugar, chopped chocolate and vanilla essence and stir until smooth.

**3** Pour the chocolate mixture into the mould and leave in a cool place for several hours to set. Turn out on to a serving plate, scatter the white and plain chocolate curls over and serve at once.

## COOK'S TIP

To unmould the blancmange, invert a large serving plate on top of the mould, then, holding plate and mould firmly together, invert both. Give both plate and mould a gentle but firm shake to loosen the blancmange, then lift off the mould.

# Ice Cream Strawberry Shortcake

This American classic couldn't be easier to make. Fresh, juicy strawberries, shop-bought flan cases and rich vanilla ice cream are all you need to create a feast of a dessert.

*Serves 4*

INGREDIENTS

3 x 15 cm/6 in sponge flan cases, or shortbread rounds
1.2 litres/2 pints/5 cups vanilla or strawberry ice cream
675 g/1½ lb hulled fresh strawberries, halved if large

*strawberries*

*vanilla ice cream*

*flan case*

**1** If using flan cases, trim the raised edges with a serrated knife.

**2** Set aside a third of the ice cream and strawberries for the topping. Place half the remaining ice cream and strawberries on one flan case or shortbread.

**3** Place a second flan case on top and cover with a second layer of ice cream and fruit.

**4** Top with the third flan case, the reserved ice cream and strawberries and serve.

## COOK'S TIP

Don't worry if the shortcake falls apart when you cut into it. Messy cakes are best. Ice Cream Strawberry Shortbread can be assembled up to 1 hour in advance and kept in the freezer without spoiling the fruit.

# Summer Pudding

This traditional British pudding is such a perfect way of presenting soft fruits that it has been widely exported and is now popular wherever berries grow.

*Serves 6–8*

INGREDIENTS

1 loaf of white farmhouse-type
  bread, 1–2 days old, sliced
675 g/1½ lb fresh redcurrants
75 g/3 oz/6 tbsp granulated sugar
60 ml/4 tbsp water
675 g/1½ lb mixed berries, such as
  raspberries, blueberries and
  blackberries
juice of ½ lemon
whipped cream, to serve (optional)

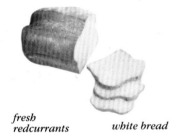

*fresh
redcurrants*          *white bread*

*mixed berries*        *granulated
                        sugar*

*lemon*

**1** Trim the crusts from the bread slices. Cut a round of bread to fit in the bottom of a 1.5 litre/2½ pint/6¼ cup domed pudding basin or mixing bowl. Line the sides of the basin with bread slices, cutting them to fit and overlapping them slightly. Reserve enough bread slices to cover the top of the basin.

**2** String the redcurrants if necessary. Mix them with 50 g/2 oz/¼ cup of the sugar and the water in a non-reactive saucepan. Heat gently, crushing the berries lightly to help the juices to flow. When the sugar has dissolved, process the currant mixture in a food processor until quite smooth. Press through a fine-mesh nylon strainer set over a bowl.

**3** One at a time, remove the shaped bread pieces from the basin and dip in the redcurrant purée. Replace to line the basin evenly. Put the mixed berries in a separate bowl. Add the remaining sugar and the lemon juice. Stir well, then spoon into the lined basin.

**5** To turn the pudding out, remove the weights, plate and clear film. Run a knife between the basin and the pudding to loosen it. Invert a serving plate on top of the pudding, then invert basin and plate together. Lift off the basin. Serve the pudding in wedges, with whipped cream if you like.

**4** Dip the reserved cut bread slices in the redcurrant purée and fit them on top of the pudding. Cover with clear film. Set a small plate, just big enough to fit inside the rim of the basin, on top of the pudding. Weigh it down with cans of food. Chill for 8 hours.

## COOK'S TIP

It is important to use good-quality bread for this dish. Ready-sliced white bread produces a disappointing result in terms of both flavour and texture.

# Eton Mess

When parents and pupils picnic on the lawns at England's Eton College as part of the annual prizegiving celebrations in early June, this dessert always gets full marks.

*Serves 4*

INGREDIENTS
500 g/1¼ lb hulled strawberries, chopped
45–60 ml/3–4 tbsp Kirsch
300 ml/½ pint/1¼ cups double cream
6 small white meringues
mint sprigs, to decorate

*strawberries*

*Kirsch*

*double cream*

*meringues*

**1** Put the strawberries in a bowl, sprinkle over the Kirsch, then cover and chill for 2–3 hours.

**2** Whip the cream until soft peaks form, then gently fold in the strawberries with their juices.

**3** Crush the meringues into rough chunks, then scatter them over the strawberry mixture and fold in gently.

**4** Spoon the strawberry mixture into a glass serving bowl, decorate with mint sprigs and serve immediately.

## COOK'S TIP

For a less rich version of this delectable dessert, use strained Greek yogurt or thick natural yogurt instead of part or all of the cream. Simply beat the yogurt gently before adding the strawberries.

# Peach Melba

In the original dish created by Escoffier for the opera singer Dame Nellie Melba, peaches and ice cream were served upon an ice swan.

*Serves 4*

INGREDIENTS
300 g/11 oz hulled raspberries
squeeze of lemon juice
icing sugar, to taste
2 large ripe peaches or 425 g/15 oz
    can sliced peaches
8 scoops vanilla ice cream

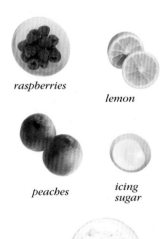

*raspberries*

*lemon*

*peaches*

*icing sugar*

*vanilla ice cream*

**1** Press the raspberries through a fine-mesh nylon strainer set over a bowl. Stir in a little lemon juice and sweeten to taste with icing sugar.

**2** If using fresh peaches, dip them in boiling water for 4–5 seconds, then slip off the skins. Cut them in half along the indented line, then slice them. If using canned peaches, drain them well.

**3** Place two scoops of ice cream in each individual glass dish, top with peach slices, then pour over the raspberry purée. Serve immediately.

## COOK'S TIP
If you'd like to prepare this ahead of time, scoop the ice cream on to a cold baking sheet and freeze until ready to serve, then transfer the scoops to the dishes.

# SOUFFLÉS, CUSTARDS & CRÊPES

## Frozen Grand Marnier Soufflés

Simple yet sophisticated, frozen soufflés make an excellent dinner party dessert as they can be prepared well ahead.

### Serves 8

INGREDIENTS
225 g/8 oz/1 cup caster sugar
6 large eggs, separated
250 ml/8 fl oz/1 cup milk
15 g/½ oz powdered gelatine,
    dissolved in 45 ml/3 tbsp water
    until spongy
475 ml/16 fl oz/2 cups double cream
60 ml/4 tbsp Grand Marnier

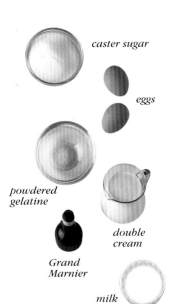

*caster sugar*

*eggs*

*powdered gelatine*

*double cream*

*Grand Marnier*

*milk*

**1** Tie a double collar of greaseproof paper around eight ramekin dishes. Put 75 g/3 oz/6 tbsp of the sugar in a bowl with the egg yolks and whisk until pale.

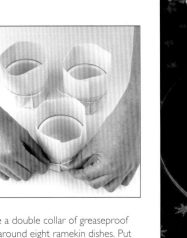

**2** Heat the milk until almost boiling and pour it on to the egg yolk mixture, whisking all the time. Return to the pan and stir over a gentle heat until thick enough to coat the spoon. Remove from the heat and stir in the sponged gelatine until dissolved. Pour the custard into a bowl and leave to cool. Whisk occasionally, until on the point of setting.

**3** Put the remaining sugar in a pan with 45 ml/3 tbsp water and dissolve it over a low heat. Bring to the boil and boil rapidly until it reaches the soft ball stage or 118°C/240°F on a sugar thermometer. Remove from the heat. In a grease-free bowl, whisk the egg whites until they are stiff. Pour on the hot syrup, whisking all the time. Leave to cool.

**4** Whisk the cream until it holds soft peaks. Add the Grand Marnier to the cold custard, then fold the custard into the cold meringue, with the cream. Quickly spoon into the prepared ramekin dishes. Freeze overnight. Remove the paper collars. Leave the soufflés at room temperature for 30 minutes before serving.

# Apple Soufflé Omelette

Apples sautéed until they are slightly caramelized make a delicious filling for an omelette dredged with icing sugar and branded with a hot skewer.

## Serves 2

INGREDIENTS
4 eggs, separated
30 ml/2 tbsp single cream
15 ml/1 tbsp caster sugar
15 g/½ oz/1 tbsp butter
icing sugar, for dredging

FOR THE FILLING
25 g/1 oz/2 tbsp butter
1 eating apple, peeled, cored and sliced
30 ml/2 tbsp soft light brown sugar
45 ml/3 tbsp single cream

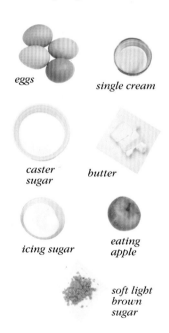

*eggs*

*single cream*

*caster sugar*

*butter*

*icing sugar*

*eating apple*

*soft light brown sugar*

**1** Make the filling. Melt the butter in a frying pan. Add the apples and sprinkle them with the brown sugar. Sauté until the apples are just tender and have caramelized a little. Stir in the cream and keep warm while making the omelette.

**2** Place the egg yolks in a bowl. Add the cream and sugar and beat well. In a grease-free bowl whisk the egg whites until they hold soft peaks, then fold them into the yolk mixture.

**3** Preheat the grill. Melt the butter in a large, heavy-based frying pan. Pour in the soufflé mixture and spread evenly. Cook for 1 minute until golden underneath, then place the pan under the hot grill to brown the top of the omelette.

**4** Heat a metal skewer. Slide the omelette on to a plate, add the apple mixture, then fold it over. Sift the icing sugar over thickly, then mark in a criss-cross pattern with a hot metal skewer. Serve immediately.

# Mocha Cream Pots

The name of this rich, baked custard, a traditional French chocolate dessert, comes from the baking cups, called *pots de crème*.

## *Serves 8*

INGREDIENTS
475 ml/16 fl oz/2 cups milk
15 ml/1 tbsp instant coffee powder
75 g/3 oz/6 tbsp caster sugar
225 g/8 oz plain chocolate, chopped
10 ml/2 tsp vanilla essence
30 ml/2 tbsp coffee-flavour
  liqueur (optional)
7 egg yolks
whipped cream and crystallized
  mimosa balls, to decorate

*milk*

*instant coffee powder*

*caster sugar*

*plain chocolate*

*vanilla essence*

*egg yolks*

*coffee-flavour liqueur*

**1** Preheat the oven to 160°C/325°F/Gas 3. Place eight 120 ml/4 fl oz/½ cup *pots de crème* cups or ramekins in a roasting tin. Heat the milk with the instant coffee powder and sugar, whisking until both the coffee and the sugar have dissolved.

**2** Remove the pan from the heat and add the chocolate. Stir until the chocolate has melted and the sauce is smooth. Stir in the vanilla essence and coffee-flavour liqueur, if using.

**3** Whisk the egg yolks lightly in a bowl, slowly whisk in the chocolate mixture until well blended, then strain the mixture into a large jug and divide equally among the cups or ramekins in the roasting tin. Pour in enough boiling water to come half-way up the sides of the cups or ramekins. Cover with foil.

**4** Bake for 30–35 minutes until the custards are just set and a knife inserted into one of them comes out clean. Remove the cups or ramekins from the roasting tin and allow to cool. Place on a baking sheet, cover and chill. Just before serving, decorate with whipped cream and crystallized mimosa balls.

# Crème Caramel

The contrast between rich, dark caramel and creamy custard ensures that this classic French dessert will never lose its popularity.

*Serves 4–6*

INGREDIENTS
115 g/4 oz/½ cup granulated sugar
60 ml/4 tbsp water
300 ml/½ pint/1¼ cups milk
300 ml/½ pint/1¼ cups single cream
6 eggs
75 g/3 oz/6 tbsp caster sugar
2.5 ml/½ tsp vanilla essence

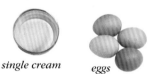
*granulated sugar*

*milk*

*single cream*

*eggs*

*caster sugar*

*vanilla essence*

**1** Preheat the oven to 150°C/300°F/ Gas 2. Half-fill a large roasting tin with water. Place the granulated sugar in a heavy-based saucepan with the water and heat gently, swirling the pan occasionally, until the sugar has dissolved. Increase the heat and boil to a rich caramel colour. Carefully pour the caramel into an ovenproof soufflé dish. Place in the roasting tin and set aside.

## COOK'S TIP
Don't be tempted to use a shallow plate for serving the crème caramel or the sauce will overflow it.

**2** Heat the milk and cream together in a pan until almost boiling. Meanwhile, whisk the eggs with the caster sugar and vanilla essence. Whisk the hot milk into the egg mixture.

**3** Strain the mixture into the caramel-coated soufflé dish and bake for 1½–2 hours (topping up the water level after 1 hour), until the custard has set in the centre. Lift the dish carefully out of the water and leave to cool, then cover and chill overnight.

**4** Loosen the sides of the chilled custard with a knife. Invert a deep plate on top. Holding the dish and plate together, turn upside down and give the whole thing a quick shake to release the crème caramel.

# Crème Brûlée

This dessert actually originated in Cambridge, England, but has become associated with France and is widely eaten there. Add a little liqueur, if you like, but it is equally delicious without it.

## Serves 6

INGREDIENTS
1 vanilla pod
1 litre/1¾ pints/4 cups double cream
6 egg yolks
115 g/4 oz/½ cup caster sugar
30 ml/2 tbsp almond- or orange-
   flavour liqueur
75 g/3 oz/½ cup soft light
   brown sugar

*vanilla pod*

*double cream*

*caster sugar*

*egg yolks*

*orange-flavour liqueur*

*soft light brown sugar*

**1** Preheat the oven to 150°C/300°F/ Gas 2. Place six 120 ml/4 fl oz/½ cup ramekins in a roasting tin and set aside.

**2** With a small knife, split the vanilla pod lengthways and scrape the seeds into a saucepan. Add the pod and the cream and bring to the boil. Remove from the heat and cover. Leave to stand for 15–20 minutes. Remove the pod.

**3** In a bowl, whisk the egg yolks with the caster sugar and liqueur. Whisk in the hot cream and strain into a large jug. Divide the custard among the ramekins.

**4** Pour enough boiling water into the roasting tin to come half-way up the sides of the ramekins. Cover the tin with foil and bake for about 30 minutes until the custards are just set. Remove from the tin and leave to cool. Return to the dry roasting tin and chill.

**5** Preheat the grill. Sprinkle the sugar evenly over the surface of each custard and grill for 30–60 seconds until the sugar melts and caramelizes. (Do not let the sugar burn or the custard curdle.) Place in the refrigerator to set the crust and chill completely before serving.

## COOK'S TIP

To test whether the custards are ready, push the point of a knife into the centre of one – if it comes out clean, the custards are cooked.

# Cherry Pancakes

You can toss these together in next to no time, using storecupboard ingredients.

*Serves 4*

INGREDIENTS
50 g/2 oz/½ cup plain flour
50 g/2 oz/⅓ cup wholemeal flour
pinch of salt
1 egg white
150 ml/¼ pint/⅔ cup milk
150 ml/¼ pint/⅔ cup water
oil, for frying

FOR THE FILLING
425 g/15 oz can black cherries
     in juice
7.5 ml/1½ tsp arrowroot

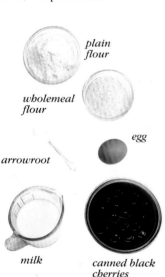

*plain flour*

*wholemeal flour*

*egg*

*arrowroot*

*milk*

*canned black cherries*

**1** Sift the flours and salt into a bowl. Tip in any bran remaining in the sieve.

**2** Make a well in the centre of the flour mixture and add the egg white. Gradually beat in the milk and water, whisking hard until all the liquid has been incorporated and the batter is smooth and bubbly.

**3** Heat a small amount of oil in a non-stick pancake pan until very hot. Pour in just enough batter to cover the bottom, swirling the pan to make an even pancake.

**4** Cook until the pancake is set and golden, and then turn to cook the other side. Slide on to a sheet of kitchen paper. Cook the remaining batter in the same way, to make eight pancakes in all.

**5** Drain the cherries, reserving the juice. Pour about 30 ml/2 tbsp of the juice into a small saucepan and stir in the arrowroot, then stir in the rest of the juice. Heat gently, stirring, until the mixture boils, thickens and clears.

**6** Add the cherries and stir until hot. spoon the cherry filling into the pancakes and fold them in quarters. Serve at once.

## COOK'S TIP
Use fresh cherries if they are in season. Cook them gently in enough apple juice just to cover them, then thicken the juice with arrowroot as in the recipe.

# Chocolate Crêpes with Plum and Port

Crêpes are a time-honoured treat. They can be served very simply or, as in this case, shoot to stardom with a superb filling and sauce.

*Serves 6*

INGREDIENTS
50 g/2 oz plain chocolate, broken
 into squares
200 ml/7 fl oz/scant 1 cup milk
120 ml/4 fl oz/½ cup single cream
30 ml/2 tbsp cocoa powder
115 g/4 oz/1 cup plain flour
2 eggs
oil, for frying

FOR THE FILLING
500 g/1¼ lb red or golden plums
50 g/2 oz/¼ cup caster sugar
30 ml/2 tbsp water
30 ml/2 tbsp port
175 g/6 oz/¾ cup crème fraîche

FOR THE SAUCE
150 g/5 oz plain chocolate, broken
 into squares
175 ml/6 fl oz/¾ cup double cream
30 ml/2 tbsp port

*plain chocolate*  *milk*  *single cream*  *cocoa powder*

*plain flour*  *eggs*  *red plums*  *caster sugar*

*port*  *crème fraîche*  *double cream*

**1** In a pan over gentle heat, dissolve the chocolate in the milk. Pour into a blender or food processor with the cream, cocoa powder, flour and eggs. Process until smooth, then chill for 30 minutes.

**2** Meanwhile, make the filling. Halve and stone the plums. Place them in a saucepan and add the caster sugar and water. Bring to the boil, then lower the heat, cover and gently simmer for about 10 minutes or until the plums are tender. Stir in the port; simmer for a further 30 seconds. Remove from the heat and keep warm.

**3** Heat a crêpe pan, grease it with a little oil, then pour in just enough batter to cover the base, swirling to coat evenly. Cook until the crêpe has set, then flip it over to cook the other side. Slide the crêpe out on to a sheet of non-stick baking paper, then cook 9–11 more crêpes in the same way.

**4** Make the sauce. Combine the chocolate and cream in a saucepan. Heat gently, stirring until smooth. add the port and heat gently, stirring, for 1 minute.

**5** Divide the plum filling between the crêpes, add a dollop of crème fraîche to each and roll them up carefully. Serve in individual bowls, with the chocolate sauce spooned over the top.

## COOK'S TIP
Vary the fruit according to what is in season, using a complementary liqueur or spirit. Try cherries with cherry brandy, mandarin orange segments with Grand Marnier or poached pears or apples with Calvados. All will taste wonderful with chocolate.

# Crêpes Suzette

This famous French dessert is easy to make at home. You can cook the crêpes in advance, ready to assemble the dish at the last minute.

*Serves 6*

INGREDIENTS
115 g/4 oz/1 cup plain flour
1.5 ml/¼ tsp salt
25 g/1 oz/2 tbsp caster sugar
2 eggs, lightly beaten
250 ml/8 fl oz/1 cup milk
60 ml/4 tbsp water
60 ml/4 tbsp orange-flavour liqueur
25 g/1 oz/2 tbsp butter, melted, plus
   extra for frying
30 ml/2 tbsp brandy, for flaming
orange segments, to decorate

FOR THE ORANGE SAUCE
75 g/3 oz/6 tbsp butter
50 g/2 oz/¼ cup caster sugar
grated rind and juice of 1 large orange
grated rind and juice of 1 lemon
150 ml/¼ pint/⅔ cup fresh orange
   juice
60 ml/4 tbsp orange-flavour liqueur,
   plus extra for flaming

*plain flour*

*caster sugar*

*eggs*

*milk*

*orange-flavour liqueur*

*butter*

*orange*

*lemon*

*brandy*

*orange juice*

**1** Sift together the flour and salt into a bowl. Stir in the sugar. Make a well in the centre and pour in the beaten eggs. Whisk vigorously, gradually incorporating the surrounding flour mixture. Whisk in the milk and water to make a smooth batter. Whisk in half the liqueur, then strain the batter into a large jug and set aside for 20–30 minutes.

**4** Make the sauce. Melt the butter in a large frying pan, then stir in the sugar, orange and lemon rind and juice, the additional orange juice and the orange liqueur.

**2** Heat an 18 cm/7 in crêpe pan. Stir the melted butter into the crêpe batter. Brush the hot pan with a little extra melted butter and pour in about 30 ml/ 2 tbsp batter. Tilt the pan to cover the base thinly. Cook the crêpe until the top is set and the base is golden, then turn it over and cook for 20–30 seconds, just to set. Slide out on to a plate.

**3** Continue cooking the crêpes, stirring the batter occasionally and brushing the pan with a little melted butter as needed. Place a sheet of clear film between each crêpe as they are stacked to prevent them from sticking. (Crêpes can be prepared ahead to this point – wrap and chill until ready to use.)

**5** Place a crêpe in the pan, browned-side down, and swirl to coat with sauce. Fold in half twice to form a triangle. Push to the side of the pan. Continue heating and folding the crêpes until all are warm and covered with the sauce.

**6** To flame the crêpes, heat the remaining orange liqueur with the brandy in a small saucepan. Remove from the heat. Carefully ignite the liquid, then gently pour it over the crêpes. Scatter over the orange segments and serve.

# FESTIVE PUDDINGS

## Round Christmas Pudding

Traditionally, Christmas puddings were cooked in a cloth suspended in boiling water, and looked like cannonballs. Modern moulds make it easy to reproduce the authentic shape.

### *Makes 1 large or 2 small puddings*

INGREDIENTS

50 g/2 oz/4 tbsp butter, melted, plus extra for greasing
350 g/12 oz/1½ cups mixed dried fruit
200 g/7 oz/1 cup mixed dried fruit salad, chopped
50 g/2 oz/½ cup flaked almonds
1 small carrot, coarsely grated
1 small cooking apple, peeled and coarsely grated
grated rind and juice of 1 lemon
15 ml/1 tbsp black treacle
90 ml/6 tbsp stout
50 g/2 oz/1 cup fresh white breadcrumbs
50 g/2 oz/½ cup plain flour
5 ml/1 tsp ground allspice
50 g/2 oz/⅓ cup dark soft brown sugar
1 egg
holly sprigs, to decorate (optional)

*butter*

*mixed dried fruit salad*

*flaked almonds*

*carrot*

*mixed dried fruit*

*cooking apple*

*lemon*

*black treacle*

*fresh white breadcrumbs*

*plain flour*

*dark soft brown sugar*

*allspice*

*egg*

**1** Lightly butter a 13 cm/5 in round Christmas pudding mould or two 7.5 cm/3 in moulds, and place a disc of non-stick baking paper in the base of each half. Have a saucepan ready into which the pudding mould(s) will fit.

**2** Mix all the dried fruits, nuts, carrot and apple in a large mixing bowl. Stir in the lemon rind and juice, treacle and stout until well blended. Cover with clear film and leave in a cool place for a few hours or overnight.

**3** Add the breadcrumbs. Sift in the flour, then stir in the allspice, sugar, melted butter and egg. Mix well. Spoon the mixture into both halves of the mould(s) so they are evenly filled.

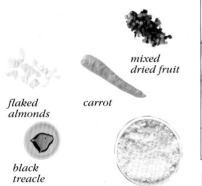

**4** Place both halves of the mould(s) together, stand on the base and clip firmly together to secure during cooking. Carefully place in the saucepan. Half-fill the pan with boiling water, taking care that the water does not reach any higher than the join of the mould(s).

**5** Bring to the boil, lower the heat, cover and simmer very gently for 5–6 hours, replenishing the saucepan with boiling water as needed. Carefully lift off the top half of the mould(s) and leave until the pudding is cold. Turn out and decorate with holly, if you like.

# Mini Black Buns

Black bun is a traditional Scottish recipe with a fruit cake mixture cooked inside a pastry case. This variation uses marzipan instead of pastry.

## *Makes 4*

INGREDIENTS
50 g/2 oz/4 tbsp butter, melted, plus
    extra for brushing
225 g/8 oz/1 cup mixed dried fruit
50 g/2 oz/¼ cup glacé cherries,
    chopped
50 g/2 oz/½ cup chopped almonds
10 ml/2 tsp grated lemon rind
25 g/1 oz/2 tbsp caster sugar
15 ml/1 tbsp whisky
50 g/2 oz/½ cup plain flour, sifted
5 ml/1 tsp mixed spice
1 egg, beaten

FOR THE DECORATION
75 ml/5 tbsp apricot jam
5 ml/1 tsp water
450 g/1 lb white marzipan
purple and green food colouring

mixed dried fruit

butter

chopped almonds

glacé cherries

grated lemon rind

caster sugar

apricot jam

plain flour

egg

whisky

white marzipan

**1** Preheat the oven to 150°C/300°F/ Gas 2. Cut out four 15 cm/6 in squares of greaseproof paper and four squares of foil. Place the greaseproof paper squares on top of the foil squares and brush with a little melted butter.

**2** Mix the dried fruit, cherries, chopped almonds, lemon rind, sugar, whisky, sifted flour and mixed spice in a large mixing bowl. Stir well. Add the melted butter and egg and beat together until well blended.

**3** Divide the mixture among the four squares, draw up the edges to the centre and twist to mould the mixture into rounds. Place on a baking sheet and bake for 45 minutes or until the mixture feels firm when touched. Remove the foil and bake for 15 minutes more. Open the paper and cool the buns on a wire rack.

**4** Heat the apricot jam and water in a small pan, then press through a strainer into a bowl. Remove the paper from the buns and brush each one with the apricot glaze. Cut off a quarter of the marzipan for decoration and put to one side. Cut the remainder into four pieces.

**5** Roll out each piece of marzipan thinly and cover the cakes, tucking the joins underneath. Roll each cake in the palms of your hands to make them into round shapes. Preheat the grill. Place the cakes on a baking sheet lined with foil.

**6** Grill the cakes until the marzipan is evenly browned. Leave until cold. Colour half the reserved marzipan purple and half green. Cut out four purple thistle shapes, green leaves and stems and arrange them on top of each cake, moistening with a little water to stick.

# Chocolate and Chestnut Yule Log

This is based on the French *bûche de Noël*, a traditional Christmas treat. It freezes well and is an excellent dessert for a party.

## *Serves 8*

INGREDIENTS
25 g/1 oz/¼ cup plain flour
30 ml/2 tbsp cocoa powder
pinch of salt
3 large eggs, separated
large pinch of cream of tartar
115 g/4 oz/½ cup caster sugar, plus extra to dust
2–3 drops almond essence
sifted cocoa powder and holly sprigs, to decorate

FOR THE FILLING
15 ml/1 tbsp brandy
5 ml/1 tsp powdered gelatine
115 g/4 oz dark chocolate, broken into squares
50 g/2 oz/¼ cup caster sugar
250 g/9 oz canned chestnut purée
300 ml/½ pint/1¼ cups double cream

plain flour

cocoa powder

eggs

cream of tartar

caster sugar

almond essence

brandy

powdered gelatine

dark chocolate

canned chestnut purée

double cream

**1** Preheat the oven to 180°C/350°F/ Gas 4. Grease and line a 33 x 23 cm/ 13 x 9 in Swiss roll tin and line the base with non-stick baking paper. Sift the flour, cocoa and salt on to a piece of greaseproof paper.

**2** Whisk the egg whites in a large, grease-free bowl until frothy. Add the cream of tartar and whisk again until stiff. Gradually whisk in half the caster sugar, until the mixture will stand in stiff peaks.

**3** Put the egg yolks and the remaining sugar in another bowl and whisk until thick. Add the almond essence. Stir in the sifted flour and cocoa mixture. Lastly, fold in the egg whites, using a metal spoon, until everything is evenly blended.

**4** Spoon the mixture into the Swiss roll tin and level the top. Bake for 15–20 minutes. Turn the Swiss roll on to a sheet of greaseproof paper dusted with caster sugar, remove the lining paper, and roll up the roll with the greaseproof paper still inside. Cool on a wire rack.

**5** Make the filling. Put the brandy in a cup and sprinkle over the powdered gelatine; leave until spongy. Melt the chocolate in a medium-sized heatproof bowl over a pan of hot water. Melt the sponged gelatine over hot water and add to the chocolate. Stir well.

 With an electric beater, whisk in the sugar and chestnut purée. Remove from the heat and leave to cool. Whisk the cream until it holds soft peaks. Fold the two mixtures together. Unroll the cake, spread it with half the filling and roll it up again. Place it on a serving dish and spread over the rest of the chocolate cream to cover. Mark it with a fork to resemble a log. Chill until firm. Dust the cake with sifted cocoa powder and decorate the plate with sprigs of holly.

## COOK'S TIP

Small decorative 'mushrooms' are traditionally used to enhance the chocolate yule log. These can be made from meringue. Pipe the 'caps' and 'stems' separately, and when dry, stick together using a little ganache or melted chocolate.

# De Luxe Mincemeat Tart

Mince pies and tarts have been traditional Christmas treats for centuries. The mincemeat can be made up in advance and kept in the refrigerator for up to two weeks.

*Serves 8*

INGREDIENTS
225 g/8 oz/2 cups plain flour
10 ml/2 tsp ground cinnamon
50 g/2 oz/½ cup walnuts, finely
    ground
115 g/4 oz/½ cup butter
50 g/2 oz/¼ cup caster sugar, plus
    extra for dusting
1 egg
2 drops vanilla essence
15 ml/1 tbsp cold water

FOR THE MINCEMEAT
2 eating apples, peeled, cored and
    coarsely grated
225 g/8 oz/1⅓ cups raisins
115 g/4 oz ready-to-eat dried
    apricots, chopped
115 g/4 oz ready-to-eat dried figs or
    prunes, chopped
225 g/8 oz green grapes, halved
    and seeded
50 g/2 oz/½ cup chopped almonds
finely grated rind of 1 lemon
30 ml/2 tbsp lemon juice
30 ml/2 tbsp brandy
1.5 ml/¼ tsp mixed spice
115 g/4 oz/⅔ cup soft light
    brown sugar
25 g/1 oz/2 tbsp butter, melted

*flour*

*cinnamon*

*chopped walnuts*

*butter*

*caster sugar*

*egg*

*vanilla essence*

*eating apple*

*raisins*

*dried apricots*

*dried figs*

*grapes*

*almonds*

*lemon*

*brandy*

*soft light brown sugar*

**1** Put the flour, cinnamon, walnuts and butter in a food processor. Process until the mixture resembles fine breadcrumbs. Tip into a bowl and stir in the sugar. Beat the egg with the vanilla essence and water. Gradually stir the egg mixture into the dry ingredients to make a soft, pliable dough. Knead until smooth, then wrap in clear film and chill for 30 minutes.

**2** Mix all the mincemeat ingredients together thoroughly in a bowl.

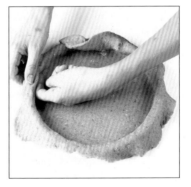

**3** Cut one-third off the pastry and reserve it for the lattice. Roll out the remainder and use it to line a 23 cm/9 in loose-based flan tin. Push the pastry well into the edges and make a 5 mm/¼ in rim around the top edge.

**4** With a rolling pin, roll off the excess pastry to neaten the edge. Fill the pastry case with the mincemeat.

**5** Roll out the remaining pastry and cut it into 1 cm/½ in strips. Arrange the strips in a lattice over the top of the pastry, wet the joins and press them together well. Chill for 30 minutes.

**6** Preheat the oven to 190°C/375°F/ Gas 5. Place a baking sheet in the oven to preheat. Brush the pastry with water and dust it with caster sugar. Bake the tart on the baking sheet for 30–40 minutes. Transfer to a wire rack. Cool for 15 minutes, then carefully remove the flan tin. Serve warm or cold.

# Iced Praline Torte

Make this elaborate torte several days ahead, and keep it in the freezer until you are ready to serve it.

*Serves 8*

INGREDIENTS
115 g/4 oz/1 cup almonds or
   hazelnuts
115 g/4 oz/½ cup caster sugar
115 g/4 oz/⅔ cup raisins
90 ml/6 tbsp brandy or rum
115 g/4 oz dark chocolate, broken
   into squares
30 ml/2 tbsp milk
475 ml/16 fl oz/2 cups double cream
30 ml/2 tbsp strong black coffee
16 sponge fingers

TO FINISH
150 ml/¼ pint/⅔ cup double cream
50 g/2 oz/½ cup almonds, toasted
15 g/½ oz dark chocolate, melted

almonds

caster sugar

brandy

raisins

dark
chocolate

milk

black
coffee

double
cream

sponge
fingers

**1** Make the praline. Put the nuts into a heavy-based pan with the sugar and heat gently until the sugar melts. Cook slowly, until the nuts brown and the sugar caramelizes. Tip on to an oiled baking sheet and leave to cool. Break up the cooled nuts and grind to a fine powder in a food processor.

**2** Soak the raisins in half the brandy or rum for an hour. Melt the chocolate with the milk in a heatproof bowl over a pan of hot water. Remove and allow to cool. Lightly grease a 1.2 litre/2 pint/5 cup loaf tin and line it with greaseproof paper.

**3** Whisk the cream in a bowl until it holds soft peaks. Whisk in the cold chocolate, then fold in the praline and the soaked raisins, with any liquid.

**4** Mix the coffee and remaining brandy or rum in a shallow dish. Dip in the sponge fingers and arrange half in a layer over the base of the prepared loaf tin.

**5** Cover with the chocolate mixture and add another layer of soaked sponge fingers. Freeze overnight.

**6** Dip the tin briefly into warm water and turn the torte out on to a serving plate. Cover and pipe with whipped cream. Sprinkle with toasted flaked almonds and drizzle the chocolate over the top. Return the torte to the freezer until needed; stand at room temperature for an hour before serving.

# Crunchy Apple and Almond Flan

Generations of cooks have taken pride in making this traditional flan, with its attractive arrangement of tender apples topped with nut crumble.

## Serves 8

INGREDIENTS
175 g/6 oz/1½ cups plain flour
75 g/3 oz/6 tbsp butter, cubed
25 g/1 oz/⅓ cup ground almonds
25 g/1 oz/2 tbsp caster sugar
1 egg yolk
15 ml/1 tbsp cold water
1.5 ml/¼ tsp almond essence
675 g/1½ lb cooking apples
25 g/1 oz/3 tbsp raisins (optional)
sifted icing sugar, to decorate

FOR THE CRUNCHY TOPPING
115 g/4 oz/1 cup plain flour
1.5 ml/¼ tsp mixed spice
50 g/2 oz/4 tbsp butter, diced
50 g/2 oz/⅓ cup demerara sugar
50 g/2 oz/½ cup flaked almonds

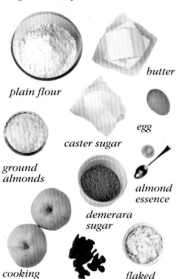

plain flour

butter

caster sugar

egg

ground almonds

almond essence

demerara sugar

cooking apples

raisins

flaked almonds

**1** Process the flour and butter in a food processor until it resembles fine breadcrumbs. Stir in the ground almonds and sugar. Whisk the egg yolk, water and almond essence together and add to the dry ingredients to form a dough. Knead lightly, wrap and leave for 20 minutes.

**2** Meanwhile, make the crunchy topping. Sift the flour and mixed spice into a bowl and rub in the butter. Stir in the sugar and almonds.

**3** Roll out the pastry on a lightly floured surface and use it to line a 23cm/9 in loose-based flan tin, taking care to press it neatly into the edges and to make a lip around the top edge. Roll off the excess pastry to neaten the edge. Chill for 15 minutes.

**6** Leave the flan to cool in the tin for 10 minutes. Serve warm or cold, dusted with sifted icing sugar.

**4** Preheat the oven to 190°C/375°F/Gas 5. Place a baking sheet in the oven to preheat. Peel, core and slice the apples thinly. Arrange in the flan case in concentric circles, doming the centre.

**5** Scatter over the raisins, if using. Cover the apples with the crunchy topping, pressing it on lightly. Bake on the hot baking sheet for 25–30 minutes, or until golden brown and the apples are tender when tested with a fine skewer.

## COOK'S TIP

Do not be tempted to put any sugar with the apples, as this makes them produce too much liquid. All the sweetness necessary is in the pastry and topping.

# Chocolate Roulade

The traditional chocolate roll takes a step into the luxury league with a wonderfully rich coconut cream filling.

## Serves 8

INGREDIENTS
150 g/5 oz/⅔ cup caster sugar
5 eggs, separated
50 g/2 oz/½ cup cocoa powder

FOR THE FILLING
300 ml/½ pint/1¼ cups double cream
45 ml/3 tbsp whisky
50 g/2 oz piece solid creamed
    coconut
30 ml/2 tbsp caster sugar

FOR THE TOPPING
coarsely grated curls of fresh
    coconut
chocolate curls

*caster sugar*

*eggs*

*cocoa powder*    *double cream*

*whisky*

*chocolate curls*

**1** Preheat the oven to 180°C/350°F/ Gas 4. Grease and line a 33 x 23 cm/ 13 x 9 in Swiss roll tin. Dust a large sheet of greaseproof paper with 30 ml/2 tbsp of the caster sugar.

**2** Whisk the egg yolks with the remaining caster sugar in a heatproof bowl until the mixture is thick enough to leave a trail. Sift the cocoa over, then fold it in carefully and evenly. Whisk the egg whites in a grease-free bowl until they form soft peaks. Fold about 15 ml/1 tbsp of the whites into the chocolate mixture to lighten it, then fold in the rest evenly.

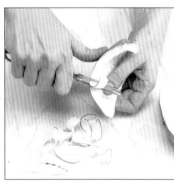

**3** Scrape the mixture into the prepared tin. Smooth the surface, then bake for 20–25 minutes or until well risen and springy to the touch. Turn out on to the sugar-dusted paper and peel off the lining paper. Cover with a damp, clean dish towel and leave to cool.

**4** Make the filling. Whip the cream with the whisky in a bowl until the mixture just holds its shape, then finely grate the creamed coconut and stir it in with the sugar.

**5** Uncover the sponge and spread with about three-quarters of the cream mixture. Roll up carefully from a long side. Transfer to a plate, pipe or spoon the remaining cream mixture on top, then decorate with the coconut and chocolate curls.

# INDEX